To God Be The Glory!
We Must Never Give Up!

TO GOD BE THE GLORY

We must never give up!

This Is My Story Growing Up Black In America

Charles A. Wiley

C.A. Wiley Publishing

ISBN: 978-1-63649-477-7

Editor: Marie Pulido
Co-Editor: Lynn Wiley

Artwork: Front and back cover by Thomas Pearson, Cincinnati, OH

Scripture reference is taken from the King James Version, Holy Bible

Author's Notes:
This book is true, as I have remembered, to the best of my knowledge. It
also has facts that are filed in public records. The names of some of the
individuals have been changed to protect their privacy.

www.nevergiveupthrive.com

From the Projects...

To Corporate America...

*To Overcoming Racial Profiling in the
Streets of Cincinnati...*

To Entrepreneurship...

Dedication

I would like to first thank God for everything he has done for my family, this world and for me. I would also like to thank God for inspiring me to write this book. I dedicate this book to the people of the world who truly understand the Power of Diversity and Change!!

"We Must Never Give Up"

Counselor, when I was a part of the problem that was hurting our community, you let me know that I needed to be a part of the solution.

We Must Never Give Up!

Messiah, you have carried me from a mighty long way. When I was stripped of my black pride and my self-esteem, you gave me back my black pride and self-esteem in a way I never could have imagined.

We Must Never Give Up!

Most High, when I was at my lowest point in my life and wanted life itself to stop, you let me know **We Must Never Give Up!**

Redeemer, when I had no hope or faith, you gave me tremendous hope and faith. When I was torn up, beaten up, kicked and knocked down and being treated like, "since you're black, all you can do for me is get back", you taught me that...

We Must Never Give Up!

Father, when my ambitions and dreams were destroyed, you restored them in a way for the world to see. **We Must Never Give Up!**

Jehovah, you let me know that "Charles, it's time for you to stand up straight, hold your head up high, and be stronger than you ever have, and put all your trust in me". **We Must Never Give Up!**

King of Kings, you taught me to be the strong proud black man that you have shaped and molded me to be. **We Must Never Give Up!**

Alpha & Omega, you taught me that I have no reason to ever be down, for we are the sons and daughters of the wonderful one, the magnificent one, the one who created the Heavens and the earth, the Prince of Peace.

"Our God"
"We Must Never Give Up"

In Loving Memory of
My Sister

Norma Jean Chisley
(A.k.a. Cookie)
November 22, 1943 – November 8, 1994
I thank you for being there
To talk to when I was
At the lowest point
In my life

Special Thanks

Elease E. Wiley (AKA Granny Goodrich)
July 18, 1924 - May 16, 2004

I would like to give thanks to Elease Wiley, my mother, for giving birth to me and for being the strong black woman she was. To my wife, Tracey, the saying speaks for itself, "behind every strong man, there is an even stronger woman". To my niece, Marie Pulido my editor, I thank you very much for the years of hard work you have put into this book alongside my wife and I. We are a great team! Last, but not least, I would like to thank my family members, my friends and the acquaintances that I have met along the way who have given me their encouragement and support. Also, to the individuals that have done wrong by me and to those that I have done wrong by. It is my hope that God has taught us all and may we have learned from our past mistakes. May God bless the readers of this book.

CONTENTS

CONTENTS

Introduction

I have always believed that everything that happens, happens for a reason.

As I look back on my life, the obstacles that I have faced sometimes overwhelm me. My problems in life started at a very early age. Growing up in the presence of drugs, black-on-black crime and the many other plagues that are tearing our communities apart made it difficult for me to maintain my focus. These problems are only symptoms of the prejudice and self-hatred that some of us have within ourselves.

Of course, we all have ups and downs in our lifetime, some more than others. It's all a part of living. It just seemed that my downs far outnumbered my ups. It was one thing after another. As I entered into corporate America, I was determined to make something of myself and do something with my life. I wasn't completely blind walking into this world. I knew walking through the door that I would have to work twice as hard as my white co-workers just to be considered as good as they were. I also knew that I would have to work four times as hard to be considered slightly better. None of my past "downs" could have possibly prepared me for what lay ahead.

As my attorney, Jim Ludwig stated, "we are now living in the 2000's." When a person is faced with discrimination within a workplace, you most likely will not hear derogatory words or statements. Management is a lot smarter than that now.

Discrimination is a lot harder to prove when there aren't any derogatory words involved. However, just because there are no derogatory words or statements being used, that does not mean that there is no discrimination or racism.

Racial profiling is one of the largest problems facing the African-American community today. Racial profiling is not just a problem for a few African-American communities; it is a nationwide problem. However, there are a large number of whites in this country that feel that racial profiling only exists on a very small scale, if it exists at all. But most of us know better. African-Americans are targeted, judged and convicted solely on the basis of their skin color. Discrimination and racism are viruses that eat at the core of our American society.

By June of 2003, the City of Cincinnati had reached record levels for black on black shootings and deaths. I would say that our communities were in a state of emergency. Some of our youth were out of control. Drug activity was high and the violence was unbelievable. Even though there were many positive things coming out of our black communities, the negative seemed to outweigh the positive. African American communities nationwide were struggling with these same issues.

My prayer is that our communities put aside their differences and come together for the good of our youth and their future. We must trust in God and believe that all things are possible for those who trust in him.

(2 Chronicles 7:14) "If my people, which are called by my name, shall humble themselves, and pray, and seek my face, and turn from their wicked ways; then will I hear from heaven, and will forgive their sin, and will heal their land."

"We Must Never Give Up!"

Chapter 1

A Strong Family

As I look back over my life, I realize that growing up in the projects in one of the largest all black communities in the nation has been a blessing. I realize that God has brought me a mighty long way. I was the type of kid who made friends easily, and I had a lot of them. I wasn't the perfect child growing up and I have to say that I encountered more than my fair share of problems. However, that probably had a lot to do with the fact that once a fire was ignited in me, I never gave up on that cause.

I was born in Cincinnati, Ohio on the 22nd day of December 1962 to Elease Wiley. My mother had moved our family to Meriana Terrace, a subsidized housing complex, in Lincoln Heights when I was around a year old. I was the youngest of ten children. I never knew my birth father, but my sibling's father, Swayne Wiley, came around quite often. He was a good man and always treated me as one of his own. This helped to fill the void left by my absent biological father. I had four older sisters and five older brothers. Although I didn't have the same father, we were 100% brother and sister; there were no halves as far as we were concerned, we were just family.

I can honestly say that I really enjoyed my life while growing up. I was a very happy child and enjoyed spending my days just doing kid things. But the good times didn't stop as a youth. Even in my adult life, I have had great happiness and joy. Never did I imagine as a young boy that my life's experiences would lead me to this point. I spent my life just trying to make it out as a "whole" individual. Looking back on my life, I sometimes wonder how I made it out in one piece and in my right mind.

Being a kid in the projects, my life was in no way a "charmed" one. Things started happening to me pretty early on. At the age of six months, my older sister Roberta who was around eleven years old at the time was ironing near the bed that I was lying on. She was keeping an eye on me and doing her daily chores. With so many children in the house, everyone had to pitch in and help my mother. As my sister turned to put away an article of clothing she had just ironed, she bumped the ironing board. The iron fell on my face and then slid down my arm stopping on my hand. I have no memory of it, of course, but the story has been told to me so many times that I can actually see it happening. At the time, the scars were pretty bad. Eventually, my face healed up pretty well, but my arm and hand still have a really nasty scar.

As a child, I was pretty self-conscious of the scars. I always thought people were looking at them, and they probably were. As time went on, I learned to live with it and it didn't bother me as much. It was just a part of me. I noticed this look my sister would always have in her eyes whenever she looked at me. As I got older, I realized that it was guilt. She felt extremely bad about what had happened to me and blamed herself. She was only eleven years old at the time and I realize accidents do happen.

A couple of months after the iron incident, I was stricken with Bronchitis Pneumonia. I was hospitalized for almost two months. It wasn't until I got much older that my mother shared with me just how close I was to death.

Being a part of a large poor family was hard and sometimes very depressing. My mother did the best she could with all of us, making sure we had what we needed. It didn't always happen though; sometimes we had no choice but to go without. At the age of eight, I remember many times eating cornflakes with no milk, using water as a substitute. Food was hard to come by in our house and we never had a lot of it, but my mom always made sure we ate. Because of my mom's poor eyesight, she wasn't able to work to support us. We depended on "The System" a lot, which back in those days, wasn't a big deal. My mom would often get food from the free store.

Our living conditions weren't the best, but mom always made sure that we were clean and that our house was neat and tidy. She took a lot of pride in that. I remember there was a time when I would be afraid to go downstairs into the kitchen at night. As soon as you flipped on the light, what seemed like a thousand roaches, would scatter for cover. It always seemed like they were heading right for me. I could never understand how a house so clean could keep so many roaches. Despite the lack of food, some hand-me-down clothes and the roach-infested apartment we all shared, I wouldn't have traded my situation for the world. I couldn't have been any more proud of my family and being a part of it.

We were a very close family, and to this day, we continue to be. We looked out for each other. If one of us was hurting, the others did whatever they could to take away the pain.

My older brother Clyde was the athlete of the family. Clyde had this amazing ability to master every sport he played; baseball, football, you name it, and he was good at it. In basketball, they use to call him "Clyde the Glyde". He taught me everything I know about sports.

Now my sister Barbara, or as the men called her "Suga Bear", was a totally different story. She was a hot little number and she knew it. She had finally reached the age where she could date, but mom wasn't letting her out of her sight. I remember the look on my sister's face, (and her date's face) when my mother shoved me out the door and told her to take me with her. It was the only way she was going on a date. I loved going out with my sister and her boyfriend. I had the best time. But my purpose was to be mom's eyes and ears and that's exactly what I was. I wouldn't be in the house a good 5 minutes before I started to rattle off what she had done and said. Heaven help her if I saw her kiss the boy. Mom would know about it before I got in the door good!

Roberta was the hard working one; she always had a job somewhere. I used to really enjoy life when she worked at restaurants. I could always count on there being food in the oven the next morning. I remember when she worked at Frisch's back during the times when they actually car-hopped on roller skates. Remember the old version of the drive through when the waitresses would come out to your car and take your order?

And then there were my brothers Monroe and Thomas! Watching those two helped me become part of what I am today. Those two were never at home at the same time. It seemed like Monroe would be in prison and Thomas would be at home, then Thomas would be in prison and Monroe would be at home. There were several times when they were in prison together. Monroe and Thomas spent more time in jail than out. Their late teens through late thirties were spent in and out of jail. I missed those guys so much growing up. I used to sit outside my mother's bedroom door and just listen to her cry until she got tired. I know she asked herself what she was doing wrong. Why couldn't her boys stay out of trouble? The truth is that she didn't do anything wrong. My brothers made the choice to let their environment and poverty control them instead of them controlling it. I promised myself that I would never give my mother a reason to cry those same tears for me.

There isn't much I can say about my brother Sam. We never spent much time together, but when we did, it was real cool. I knew that if I needed his help or anything from him, that he would be there. My sisters Norma Jean (a.k.a. Cookie) and Shirley were considerably older than I was. They already had kids my age. They were more of the mom away from home. My brother Roger, for some reason, used to scare me as a child. Roger had served two consecutive terms in the Army and fought in the Vietnam War. Roger wasn't as warm and friendly as my other brothers and sisters, but it was still good to see him when he did come home to visit, especially when he had Army trinkets for me.

My mother was a good woman. I can't really recall too many people who didn't like her. My mother was kind and very loving, but she was also very firm and believed in whipping our butts when it was necessary. My mother would take me just about everywhere she went. There were so many times that we would ride the bus downtown to shop and just hang out. My brothers and sisters always said that I was spoiled rotten and my mother was to blame. Of course they did their share of spoiling me also. I personally don't think I was that spoiled. I mean I never got both a birthday and Christmas present. So what did it matter that my birthday was the 22nd of December and Christmas was the 25th of December? In my eyes, they were two different days and they deserved two different presents. But then again, I guess my attitude back then shows you that I may have been a tad bit spoiled. I never got a birthday cake or a birthday gift, but that was all right with me because Christmas was always good for me. If I wanted to, I could open up one of my Christmas gifts on my birthday. My mom would ask me what I wanted for Christmas. No matter how little money we had, she would always make it happen. As a kid, I wasn't totally blind to how we were living and how little we had, so I made sure to never ask for anything that might have been too expensive.

"A mother's love can sometimes be a mother's silence."

Chapter 2

Being Rebellious

I'll never forget the day that I learned that Swayne Wiley wasn't my biological father. It was during the summer of 1970 and I was around eight years old. The only father I had ever known came over to the house to visit. At that time I wasn't aware of the fact that this man wasn't actually my father. As I said before, he always treated me as his own. My sister Barbara, my brother Clyde and I were outside playing when he pulled up. I said "daddy, do you have any money?" and my sister said, "my daddy ain't your daddy." Growing up, I had heard little bits and pieces to that regard, but it never really registered. No one had actually come out and said that this man wasn't my father. My brother and sister thought it was funny and started to laugh. Of course, I didn't find the humor in it; I just walked away. I don't know which hurt me more; finding out that the man I thought of as my father wasn't really my father or the fact that the brother and sister I was so close to found so much humor in hurting my feelings. Finding out this way that Swayne wasn't my father destroyed me. From that point on, I wanted to know who my biological father was.

When I asked my mother who my father was, she simply replied that she was my mother and my father. I knew that there had to be a very strong reason why my mother never told me who my biological father was. After thinking about it, this man had never tried to be a part of my life. I realized just how unwanted I was by him. At the beginning of summer vacation I had a father I loved dearly.

By the end of the summer, I had no father and knew that I would never know my biological father. My love for Swayne didn't change, but something inside me did. I couldn't look at him the same way after that. He was the only father I had ever known and he continued to treat me as his own. However, as a small boy I didn't know how to deal with the fact that he really wasn't my father.

Summer was over and school was finally starting. I was not the same kid any longer; my life had changed drastically over the summer. I entered the third grade with much attitude. I was hurt and disappointed and as far as I was concerned, the entire world was going to feel that same way.

My third grade teacher's name was Miss Lightfoot. She would have to constantly get on me about acting a fool in class. I had a little buddy in class and his name was Sid. Sid was one of the baddest kids on the block. He and I quickly became best friends.

My schoolwork was not getting done, trouble always seemed to be just around the corner and my attitude was slightly above who gives a damn. Needless to say, I failed the third grade that year. The last day of school I received my report card. That was the longest walk home ever. When I got home and my mom saw that report card, well…. I won't go into the gory details, but I know a lot of you remember back in the day when your mom would cut the cord off the iron and use it as a belt?

The projects were made up of four streets that ended in court. The first street was called "Shivers", followed by "Love", "Able" was third and "Hunter" was last. The kids on Shivers would play with the kids on Love Court but we wouldn't even think about going on the last two streets, at least not without back up in the form of an adult. It worked the same way for Able and Hunter Court. There was a large price to pay if you got caught on the wrong street at the wrong time. And if you were by yourself, you could kiss that behind of yours goodbye.

As a kid, I enjoyed putting on the boxing gloves. My next door neighbor's father kept a pair of boxing gloves. He took a liking to me and he thought I was pretty good with the gloves on. I'll never forget him. His name was Mr. Brown and he taught me everything he knew about boxing. For four years, I was unbeatable.

Sid lived on Love Court. His house was right in back of mine. I wasn't the only one repeating 3rd grade; Sid didn't make it either. The following year when I passed on to the fourth grade, I had the option of going to Robert E. Lucas Elementary instead of Lincoln Heights Elementary. Both schools were in the same Princeton High School district; the only difference was that Robert E. Lucas was a racially mixed school and Lincoln Heights Elementary was basically a black school. I decided to go to Robert E. Lucas. It was a good move for me, a real good move. Sid stayed behind at Lincoln Heights Elementary but we remained friends. It wasn't difficult to maintain this friendship, considering we lived in back of each other. Attending different schools just gave us more to talk about after school.

I would be eleven years old by the end of the 4th grade academic year. I was not only going to be the biggest in my class, but the oldest. Most of the kids were only nine years old. It was bad enough that my birthday came at the end of the year, which meant that I had to start school late, but I had to be stupid and fail the third grade. This put me two years behind my peers. My first day at Robert E. Lucas was very frightening because of the new atmosphere. I was so far behind that it was a real struggle just to maintain a passing grade. You would have thought that with the extra experience I gained by repeating third grade that I would be able to keep up pretty easily. However, this was not the case. Robert E. Lucas was very different from Lincoln Heights. I had never been around so many white people and to be thrown in class with so many at one time, I went through culture shock. My mother had always taught us to treat people the way you wanted them to treat you, but my dark skin made me extremely subconscious about my decision to change schools.

It was hard enough trying to figure out the whole "light-skinned, dark-skinned" thing that was prevalent among blacks in the 1970's, but now I was adding the white thing to it. Along with my nephew Carlos, who was six months younger than me but in the fifth grade, I would sometimes spend time at his Aunt Kay's house. Carlos was light-skinned and short. I guess you could say he fit the description of the black standard of handsome. On the other hand, I was tall and dark. The black standard of what was not handsome. Just like white folk have their standard of beauty, black folk have theirs too. Unfortunately, at that time anything darker than mocha was too dark. Anyway, Carlos and I would spend time at his Aunt's house and they would sometimes take us places. They treated us according to our color. Carlos who was lighter with nicer hair was given just about anything he wanted; time, attention, candy, you name it. Since I was darker with coarse hair, I would often get the cold treatment. Granted, I wasn't actually kin on their side of the family, but we were both kids. His family really had a way of making me feel like the ugly duckling.

When I attended Lincoln Heights Elementary, we would often study black history; particularly Martin Luther King Jr. and about the civil rights movement. I often wondered what it was about our color that so upset white people. Why did whites feel the need, or should I say obligation, to treat us so badly because of our color? It was just color; everybody had one. Not all whites were the same shade of white. Some were a little darker than others were. Adding to this was the fact that blacks had their own form of discrimination against ones skin color. If you were lighter skinned, everything was fine. If you were dark, you were often treated like the dirt under someone's foot. At least with white folks, we were actually two different races, but with black folks it was really confusing because we were all black, the same race. Some of us were just lighter than others.

I never understood. Blacks were fighting whites and their system to be treated equally. Whites felt they were better than blacks because their skin was lighter. But some of those same black people who were fighting to be considered equal with whites were condemning darker skinned blacks because they were so dark. It was hypocritical! Light-skinned blacks acted as if they were better than darker skinned blacks because they were lighter, but those same fair skinned people couldn't understand why white people thought they were better than black people because they were lighter than light-skinned and dark-skinned blacks.

While attending Robert E. Lucas I noticed there was a lot of white kids and teachers who treated a lot of the other darker skinned kids and myself better than some blacks treated us. To be clear, not all the lighter skinned blacks thought they were better than we were because they were lighter. Robert E. Lucas was truly a different experience. I felt like I had so many different issues to deal with. Sometimes it was hard to just be a child. Living in the projects and facing those daily challenges didn't help matters either.

Robert E. Lucas wasn't the only time I ventured out of my comfort zone. During the summer of 1974, my mother asked me to go to the store for bologna and bread. I was scared to death because the store was about a mile away from where we lived and the street code was that you didn't go out of your own neighborhood without back up. Now my mother was asking me to do just that. I obeyed my mom and went anyway, holding my breath and looking behind me the whole time. I would say that I was about half way to the store, about a half-mile or so away from my home when it happened. Crazy Danny Racker jumped out of the bushes and directly in my path. Not only was Danny bigger than I was, but he was clinically "ill". He had been in a mental hospital for some time. Danny asked me for all my money. To his disappointment, all I had was food stamps. The word "mad" doesn't even do justice to how Danny was feeling. Brother man was beyond upset. He hit me and the fight was on. I may have been out of my mind, but I had never run from anyone and I wasn't about to run from crazy Danny Racker. I fought back and even though I had a fat lip, bloody mouth and no food stamps, I stood my ground. I can still remember the walk home. No bread, no bologna and my hands hurt something fierce. That fight with Danny Racker was one of the hardest and scariest things I had faced at that time; even harder than going to a new school. I realized on the way home that I had done a couple of things even more important than standing my ground. The first thing was I ventured outside of the projects by myself. Secondly, even though Danny Racker jumped me, I survived. At the time, I realized these two things, but I didn't understand just how important they were.

When I got home I told my mom what had happened. Of course she did what all good moms do; she cleaned me up and sent me on my way. But remember, in the hood, things don't just drop. I could have just told one of my brothers what had happened and Danny would have gotten a butt whipping he would remember till this day. But that was never my style. I always handled things myself.

Also, in the summer of 1974, my mom told me about a summer program where I could go to Camp and that a certain community program would finance it. I agreed to go without hesitation. Imagine; time away from the projects for free! You know I said yes. You know I didn't go alone. My old "road dog" Sid went with me. It was a two-week program and we made the most out of those 14 days. The week before we were supposed to head back home, the counselors took us on a trip to the beach. I didn't know how to swim, but Sid did. Now you know I wasn't going to let my boy know that I couldn't swim. Besides, I knew how to dog paddle and I figured that would get me by.

Anyway, Sid suggested that we swim out to the floaters and I agreed. I figured I would dog paddle out, rest on the floaters and then dog paddle back in. Piece of cake. We got out there with no problem, and then it happened. The floaters were not mounted to the bottom of the lake, so when a boat came past and flipped my non-swimming behind over the side, the last thing I remember, before waking up with some white girls staring in my face, was going under water. This white girl had saved my life. I never had the chance to thank her and I always wanted to. She gave me back my life, and she was WHITE! Not all white people were bad. There were some out there who didn't care about the color of my skin, but valued my life just as they did their own. The beach was really crowded that day and Sid and I were the only ones out by the floaters. To me, it was truly a miracle that she saw I was in trouble. Now that I think about it, where in the world was Sid?

I came home from Camp in the same body, but not with the same mind. I was pretty quiet following the days after my near drowning. I didn't say much; I just kind of sat around. A couple of days after I had returned home, my mom received a phone call. I had a cousin who had also gone to Camp. He had told his parents what had happened and it was his parents calling my mother. After the phone call, my mom said that she knew why I was so quiet. She said, "You almost drowned at camp". I told her that I did but what I didn't tell her was that I was still terrified. I just kept thinking; what if that girl hadn't seen me? What if she couldn't get to me in time? I wanted my mom to give me a big hug and say something to make me feel better. She never did. In fact, that was the last conversation we ever had about what happened. I knew my mother didn't understand just how serious it was and just how frightened I was about the entire incident. She probably figured that I swam out too far and had to be helped back in. She probably never knew that I went under and was unconscious. Without the help of this girl, I wouldn't have come back home. If my mother had of known just how serious the whole incident was, she would have held me forever. I probably would never have left her sight again.

"As a growing young man, the choices that you make in life can determine your destiny."

Chapter 3

Growing Up

Football and basketball were my favorite sports. I joined the community football team called The Lincoln Heights Tigers. The head coach was Paul Blackwell. Mr. Blackwell was one of the top coaches within the city of Cincinnati. Every year, his team would go to the Superbowl and win. At that time, there were a lot of talented football players coming out of Lincoln Heights. Mr. Blackwell had coached every one of them. Lincoln Heights had its own high school up until 1971. They would always win State titles in football, basketball and wrestling. Lincoln Heights was well known for its athletic programs. Princeton High School and Lincoln Heights merged. All seventh through twelfth graders were bussed to Princeton High Schools, which made the school racially mixed, or should I say an even greater racially mixed high school. Princeton High did have a few blacks, very few. Needless to say, the mixture did wonders to enhance Princeton's athletic program. Unfortunately, due to the lack of financial resources needed, Lincoln Heights was unable to maintain qualified teachers.

It was the summer of 1979 and I was 16 years old. I was working as a supervisor for the City of Lincoln Heights Summer Program for low-income teens. I actually started working my summers for them at the age of thirteen while

I played football and basketball. The summer was winding down. The job program had given kids that worked for Lincoln Heights a summer banquet. I received a plaque for "Outstanding Worker & Supervisor".

In our house, my mother had a picture of Jesus on the wall. His hands were folded as if he was praying. I don't know how, but as I was walking past the picture, which I had done many times before, it just seemed to jump off the wall and into my hands. I'm not sure if I bumped the picture or what; I just remember the picture lying in my hands. It was like the picture was talking to me and God was telling me to "come". The feeling I had was overwhelming. I put the picture back on the wall and ran out of the house at top speed. I didn't really understand what had just happened, but I knew it was really intense. I had always believed in God, I just had never felt his presence like that before. Frankly, it was a bit too much for me to handle at the time. So much went through my mind at that time. I wasn't sure if God was trying to tell me that it was time for me to get saved, or if God was telling me he was coming to get me and it was time for me to die. The only thing I knew for sure was that it did happen and it happened for a reason. I wasn't dreaming.

As with most things that happened in my life, I put it behind me and didn't discuss it with anyone. From that point on, I always felt as if God was calling me to do something. I just wasn't sure what. Meanwhile, my buddy Sid had started getting into more trouble and although I was trying to do better and be better, Sid was still my friend. Sid started smoking cigarettes. He would always light up as we walked to the bus stop. I never tried smoking when he offered, but I did sneak one of my mother's cigarettes one day. You would have thought that I would have taken the least traumatic route to smoking, which was Sid. I say "traumatic", because if my mother had caught me smoking, especially one of her cigarettes, there would have been a lot of trauma inflicted on my backside. That was the first and last time I ever touched a cigarette. Man was I sick!

Sid was really good at football. He was a lot better than I was, and he probably could have really made something out of it. Unfortunately, Sid didn't stick with it. He quit playing after we got older. He seemed to lose interest in the sport. On the other hand, I continued on through high school. By this time, I was attending Princeton High School but would leave by my eleventh grade year to attend Live Oaks Vocational School where I studied Building Maintenance. They taught us everything that had anything to do with building a home. Live Oaks Vocational was on the East side of town. It was a joint program with Princeton and several other school districts. So even though I wasn't physically attending classes at the High School, I graduated from Princeton with a diploma and from Live Oaks with a Certificate in Building Maintenance.

The majority of the students at Live Oaks were white. Including my cousin named Daryl and myself, there were about six blacks in the entire school. Daryl was becoming one of my best friends. Sid had quit school his sophomore year and was on the slow boat to destruction. I on the other hand had been doing fine. I still had a lot of obstacles being thrown my way, but I was standing my ground. I was hanging in there. I never really thought of myself as a bad kid. Coming from the projects you had to know how to hold your own or it would be like open season on you. The other kids would have a field day.

I vividly remember my second day of school at Live Oaks, during my junior year. It was lunchtime and I was going to lunch. Daryl was already in line, so I went and got in line in front of him. This white kid standing behind Daryl said" Hey! You can't let that nigger in front of you"! Before I could even think about it, I sent him and his mouth flying over the lunch table. We both were sent to the principal's office.

Of course yours truly was going to be kicked out of school. At first glance, it looked as if my actions had been unprovoked. Regardless of what the situation was, my behavior was completely unacceptable. After explaining to the principal what had happened, it was decided that although my actions were unacceptable, it was understandable why I had reacted in the manner I had. I was allowed to stay in school; however, by this time I wasn't interested in being there anymore. I told the principal I wanted to go back to Princeton. My mother and the other kid's parents were called to the school. Things got sorted out and I gave it another try. After that day, I never was called anything other than my name. The white kid and I actually became friends. He apologized and I accepted. He told me that he didn't have much experience with blacks and "nigger" was the word that his parents used frequently to refer to blacks. Like they say, it starts at home.

In early November, Basketball season started. I was still hanging with Sid. My boy was going nowhere and didn't have a clue, but Sid was my boy. I had been offered drugs several times, and turned them down each time. There's just something about when your running buddy offers. For some reason, you just can't turn him down. Maybe it's for fear of looking like a punk. So when Sid offered me a joint, I smoked it.

It was my junior year and I guess you could say that I was pretty well known. I had all kinds of friends that I hung out with. I was in a dancing group called "Chain Reaction". We would enter dance contests all over Cincinnati and most of the time we would win. There were four of us in the group, my cousin Daryl, my two friends Mark and Calvin and myself. By my junior year in high school, I wasn't only into basketball. I was also into beer, wine and weed. If my mother had known, she would have killed me. I had a couple of friends who were selling weed in and out of school. Some of the players from the football and basketball team would hang out and get high together. Life was really changing and I was moving full speed ahead. Because I was so self-conscious about my dark skin, I started to get into girls later than most of the other guys. That all had changed. I no longer felt like the ugly duckling because I was now known as the tall, dark, handsome one with the dimples. At that time, I had about five different girls that I was seeing and man did I love it!

Throughout my younger years it seemed that you had a big "X" on your forehead if you were dark. It just seemed like the closer to white you were or looked, the better chance you had of becoming someone or accomplishing something. If you were black but had lighter skin, whites were more willing to tolerate you. I said tolerate, not accept. Back in the day, I don't think whites truly accepted any black person.

But now it was a new day. My day had finally come and I was really enjoying all the extra attention. It never really crossed my mind that I was doing the girls wrong by being a player. All I knew was that in the seventies, I was like a three-legged dog. I was something to be stared at and treated just like that. In the eighties, I was tall, dark and handsome. There was a new trend going on and I was in. DARK-SKINNED BROTHA'S WERE IN!!!!!

Even while all of this was going on in my life, I just couldn't shake the experience I had had with God a short time back. I still had the feeling that God was calling me to do something and telling me that I needed to get saved. I had always been a Christian or so I thought. I attended Church regularly, but I still felt as if I was missing something. By this time I had gotten real good at ignoring this part of my life. I still had a lot of other issues that I was dealing with and couldn't handle the spiritual world right now. I still wanted and needed to know who my father was. I would ask my mother about my father, but she never would talk much about the subject so I learned to keep this issue inside of me. It does something to you when you don't know who your father is. I promised myself that when I had kids I would be there for them no matter what.

It was my senior year, parent's night at our Varsity Basketball game. I knew that a lot of my teammates were having both their parents walk out on court with them. The whole day, I was kind of feeling down. Earlier that day before the game I asked my mother again who was my father? She said, "Charles, his name is on your birth certificate in the file box". I never told you before because I always felt that if he wanted you to know him, he would have come around". At that point, I realized that it wasn't as important to me as I thought it was. She had been a strong mother for me. I had wasted so many years wishing for something that I had all the time through my mother. It's like once she told me this, he materialized, and he became a real person. Prior to that moment, there was nothing there.

I started to look at what I did have. Truly I had been blessed. My mother had taken such good care of me all those years, all by herself. I also had a stepfather with a really large family. My stepfather's side of the family had always treated me as if I was biologically theirs. I never looked at my birth certificate. On parent's night, I took the floor with my mother with more pride than I had ever felt before.

My senior year was my best year of school. Things were going great at Live Oaks Vocational. I had a lot of friends. Even though most of them were white, they were still my friends. To top it all off, my grades were good. We were learning about everything you needed to know about building a house. By the time we graduated, we knew how to read blueprints, how to do roofing, carpentry, plumbing, flooring, drywall, painting and HVAC. We learned it all and I was really good at it. This was something that I really enjoyed.

That summer before my senior year, I had saved up enough money to buy my first car. I was pretty good at saving. It was the only way for me to get the things that I wanted. I had done the same thing when I was fourteen. I just had to have a mini bike. I saved my money from my summer job and bought it myself. When I was sixteen I wanted a motorbike so I saved and bought me one. I was always the kind of kid who went after what he wanted. I would always make it happen. That was the way my mother had brought my siblings and me up. If we wanted something, we were taught not to sit and wait for someone to do for you what you can do for yourself.

During my senior year, a lot of my friends were skipping school. If you knew for sure that you had enough credits to graduate, it seemed to be all right. I think I may have done this a couple of times, but for the most part I enjoyed school and really didn't see a reason not to go. By this time, Sid was really into drugs. We had remained friends while growing up and were like brothers to each other. Watching the choices Sid was making was really hard and upsetting for me. I really loved Sid. He was my cat. I never said anything to Sid because he was his own person and I was mine. I just didn't feel like I had the right to try and tell him how to live. Besides, I wasn't perfect. I was far from it. But I wasn't a bad person either.

Sid wasn't a bad person either. However, he was making some really bad choices. I cared about Sid. I've always taken a deep interest in the well-being of other people, even people I didn't really know. Growing up in Lincoln Heights, I've been a witness to a lot. I witnessed everything from family financial problems, family members strung out on drugs and family violence. You name it; I've seen it. Nothing much surprised me. Even though the projects had its share of darkness, there were also some really fond memories that I still carry with me today. There were a lot of hard working families in the projects who got up every morning and took care of business.

My sister Shirley lived in an area of Cincinnati called Mt. Healthy during my senior year of high school. I spent a lot of time at her house with my nephew. I had made a lot of friends who lived outside of Lincoln Heights, but most of my friends were still in Lincoln Heights. There was one guy by the name of Moe. Moe was from Forest Park but he and his family moved to Lincoln Heights when we were in the ninth grade.

Lincoln Heights had this ongoing territorial battle with Mt. Healthy and Forest Park. I remember one Christmas

Eve when kids from Lincoln Heights, Mt. Healthy and Forest Park were all at this party thrown at a club called "The Apple". Moe who lived in Lincoln Heights and this other guy from Mt. Healthy were dating the same girl, who by the way was also from Mt. Healthy. The fight was on. At least six guys from Mt. Healthy including the guy who was dating Moe's girl jumped Moe. He took a serious butt whipping that night. The fight was unbelievable, complete and utter chaos.

The very next week, some of the guys from Lincoln Heights heard about what happened Christmas Eve at The Apple and decided to do some head knocking themselves. We got together about ten carloads full of guys and rode to a party in Mt. Healthy, just looking for trouble. We found the guys that had jumped Moe the week before and waled on them. There were also some guys there from Forest Park. Since we were already there and the Forest Park crew didn't have the sense to leave when it all started, we went ahead and got two birds with one stone, so to speak. I couldn't believe that things had gone this far. Even though I was in the middle of it all, I managed not to fight anyone.

My nephew Carlos who lived in Mt. Healthy was at the party that night. He wasn't in on any of the action. Carlos was more of a ladies man back then; he really didn't have time for the fighting. Carlos was all about getting the phone number. That night, he was walking out of the party with two girls. Before I knew it, my boys from Lincoln Heights were on him. I caught them just in time. They were about to go to work on him. After all the action, Carlos asked me what was going on. I told him about the guys from Mt. Healthy that had jumped Moe. I let him know that we weren't having it. When you come to our house and jump one of us, you'd better be prepared to deal with the rest of us because we're coming (All of this talk and I didn't touch a soul). Carlos looked at me and said, "what about when you come to my house"? I told him that I would deal with that when and if I had to and that right now I was put into a position of having to defend my friends, my community and myself. They needed to know that they just couldn't walk into my community and jump on us because they felt like it. I didn't like this hardcore stance, but it was necessary. When they come to our neighborhood, if they respect us then we'll respect them. But if they come to our neighborhood looking for trouble, they must be prepared to deal with the consequences.

The feuding between Lincoln Heights, Mt. Healthy and Forest Park went on for at least another year after that. During that time, no one was shot, stabbed or lost his life. One of my friends was sent to emergency when some fool took a baseball bat to him. Back in the day, we fought with our hands. Defending yourself and your neighborhood didn't mean taking someone's life. We weren't even about that. We may not have had a lot of respect for each other as individuals, but we had respect for life in general. No one had the right to take anyone's life for any reason. If you were from Lincoln Heights, you were proud of it. It was like walking around with the big "Zone 15" on your chest. You thought you were untouchable. Lincoln Heights was considered at that time to be one of the roughest, hardcore neighborhoods in the city. If you could survive there, you had earned your respect. I never started a fight, but I never backed down or ran from one either.

"We must never give up!"

Chapter 4

Becoming A Young Man

In June of 1982 I graduated from Live Oaks Vocational and Princeton High School. I worked with my mom to earn a grant to attend Central State University even though I really didn't want to go. In my mind, there were two very good reasons for me not to go. The most important reason was my mom. She was getting older. I was the last to leave home and I didn't want to leave her at home by herself. Secondly, I just didn't have the desire. College wasn't for me. I had made it through twelve years of school and that was more than enough for me. Overall, I enjoyed school, but not enough to spend another four years at some university. Although I didn't want to go to college, my mom really wanted me to go pursue a degree. As a result, we compromised. I did go, but I chose a local school so I wouldn't have to leave home.

I started Cincinnati State Community College (formerly Cincinnati Technical College) in September of 1982. College was just as foreign to me as the first time I stepped outside of Lincoln Heights. In high school, you are told what classes you have to take so it's difficult to develop an interest in learning a particular subject. In college it was completely up to you. I didn't know what I wanted to study. The only thing I did know at that time was that I really didn't want to be there. My mom and I sat down and discussed it and we came up with "Loss Control" as a major. This dealt with fire prevention and law-enforcement. This was cool with me because it was only a two-year degree, which was two years less than the four years I thought I was going to have to spend there. Well, needless to say, I didn't even finish the two years. I dropped out of CTC right before I had completed my two-year degree program. I really missed working with my hands. My mom wasn't all that thrilled with my decision to do so, but she didn't put up much of a fuss.

I started refurbishing old homes and doing some general maintenance for Avondale housing. This was what I really enjoyed. My first lesson in the workforce? Classroom learning is seriously different from on-the-job learning. Even with all the areas of home building that we covered at Live Oaks, I still wasn't as prepared as I thought I was. The work I was doing was very different from what they had taught us in school. Sometimes I worked with my boss Joe and occasionally I worked with co-workers Reggie or Anthony, but the majority of the time I worked alone. On my lunch breaks I would read my bible.

In the early part of 1984, my stepfather had a heart attack. I can still remember how upset I was. Even though Swayne wasn't my biological father and I never lived with him, I loved him dearly and I thought of him as my father. He had always been there for me no matter what. I could count on him for anything. He was in the hospital for at least a month and a half. I remember the call we got that night telling us that he would never be coming home again. All of a sudden, he was no longer with us. It really took us by surprise because he seemed to be doing so well. He had another heart attack and died that night. He was supposed to come home the next morning. On April 24th of 1984, I lost the only father I had ever known. I was truly devastated.

I found myself getting more into the word of God. I still carried with me the feeling that God was trying to reach out to me, that he was still calling me. He had never abandoned his pursuit of me over the years and now his call was even stronger. Soon after my father's death, I yielded to God's calling. There was a church right next door to my sister Norma's house. The pastor's son was Matt. He had given his life to God back in 1982. He was also one of my close friends. I went to Matt and told him that I was ready to get saved. He took me downstairs where they held church and lead me into God's realm. The church was actually in the basement of their home (I know what you're thinking, but it really did look like a church). It had an organ and drums; there were pews. You would have never known that you were in a house unless you had entered from the upstairs. The church was called Revelation Church of God. Not only did I join this body of worship, but also to my own surprise, I became a very active faithful member.

I was about twenty-two years old at the time of my transformation, so you can imagine some of the things I was into. Once I had dedicated my life to Christ, I stopped drinking and smoking weed. I even stopped dating girls. The only thing that was on my mind was working for God. It was as if I had finally found my gift in life. Whenever I testified to someone about God, they would come to visit the church. More often than not, they would join. The small church I had first entered several months ago was growing every day. I felt like God was really using me. Like any change, it wasn't always easy. The friends I hung out with before, I didn't hang out with anymore. The only time I really saw them or talked with them was when I wanted to get the word of God in their ear. The foundation for everything I did was God. I had even started to listen to gospel music. I had really grown to love the Lord and live for him. At the time, there was a particular young lady in the church that I spent time with in Bible study. Things happen. What normally happens when you spend a lot of time with someone? One night while we were studying, we started to kiss. I stopped myself before things got too out of hand. I knew something was wrong. I had managed to suppress those feelings that I had once had for women but now they were starting to resurface and I didn't want to let lustful feelings take over. I felt like I was losing my focus with God, so I had to do something.

I went to the church and asked permission to stay at their home while I fasted. I fasted in the church for three very long, hungry days. After the three days were up, my physical body was weak and hungry. In the beginning, I couldn't eat much of anything. I thought I had gotten myself back on track. However, a couple of weeks passed by and I felt the strong calling of Budweiser, a joint and short skirts. I gave in and went right back out into the world. I left Revelation Church of God and rejoined my old church Ebenezer Second Baptist.

Shortly after I had left Revelation, just about half of the members that I had brought to the church also left. Just as quickly as I had come to God, I had found myself back out in the world. I was drinking, smoking and hanging out with my old road dogs again. Now I was confused. I just didn't get it. I had fasted and prayed for strength but it seemed as if it only made me weaker. Did God not hear me? Or was I just not prepared? Either way, I had left the church.

Since Matt and I were close friends, I felt that there was no other choice but for me to leave the church. I thought that he would be monitoring my every move. At Ebenezer, I didn't have any close friends so I knew that I wouldn't be monitored. I didn't know that this would become a habit.

A couple of months later, I found myself hanging out at a club called "Skippers" with Greg, who was an old friend of mine from the hood. We were sitting down having a drink when suddenly someone punched me in the face and hit Greg in the head with an ashtray. Blood from Greg's head was everywhere and I was on the floor out cold. My sister Barbara was in the bar that night. She and Greg helped to get me up off the floor. When I came around and asked what had happened, they told me that a guy had hit us and ran out of the club. My sister and Greg asked me if I had done anything to this guy and I told them no. I didn't even know the guy.

The next day, Greg came over to my house. He had found out that the mysterious guy from the club was Reggie. He and his family were from Lincoln Heights but they lived in Wyoming, a small community about two miles outside of Lincoln Heights. Greg said that if I wanted to let Reggie get away with what he had done that it was fine with him, but he wasn't going to let him. Greg was the kind of guy who always carried a gun. I knew what might happen if he ever ran into Reggie again, and I knew he would. He was going to put some serious pain on him. Once I saw the gun Greg was carrying, I knew this wasn't going to be one of my small childhood fights. I set there quietly asking myself why and how do I always seem to get myself in the middle of this kind of drama. I didn't know Reggie and hadn't done anything to the man. Yet, here I sat looking at a gun and listening to Greg talk about what he's going to do with that gun.

I never tried to carry myself as a tough guy. I was never one to start a fight or go looking for trouble. I was a pretty laid back person. I suggested to Greg that we should just let this go. Greg's response? Typical. "Hell no!! I'll look like a punk!" "Nobody does that to me and gets away with it!" I had grown up with Greg, so I knew his words were serious. I was getting a real bad vibe.

About a week later, Greg, some friends and I went out skating. That night, Reggie and his friends happen to be there. Greg told me that he was going to get Reggie. I advised him not to do anything right away because the police were there. My words fell on deaf ears; Greg and Reggie fought anyway. You can mess with a lot of things in life, but you don't mess with a man's pride. The police broke the fight up and were holding Greg as a crowd of people gathered. I saw Reggie running towards Greg with a skate in his hand. Since the police were holding Greg, there was no way he could defend himself. It was "Super Brotha" to the rescue. I kicked off my skates and intercepted Reggie with a punch to the face.

Needless to say, all three of us were ordered to leave the premises that night. Reggie let it be known, in front of the police that Greg and I were going to pay. After a brief argument, we all went on our way. On our way out, Greg told me that I needed to get a gun to protect myself. We found out just how serious Reggie was. As it turned out, he belonged to a gang. Even though I knew better, I got a gun.

About a week later, we were at Mr. Kelly's nightclub. I was with about ten of my friends. Reggie was there with his friends. You can guess what was about to go down next. Before we could get anything started, the bouncers and police let us know that it would be in our best interest to leave and do it quickly.

The very next day, outside of my house Reggie and one of his buddies jumped me as I was on my way to get in my car. I had left my gun in the house and it's a good thing. My life would be drastically different if I had had that gun on me that day. During the fight, I took a pair of brass knuckles to the back of my head and several blows from the crowbar that Reggie's friend was swinging. Someone saw the fight and called the police and ambulance. I ended up in emergency getting several stitches to the back of my head. I was sore, bruised and had one terrible headache, but I had survived. I was still on my feet. I later filed a warrant on Reggie. The whole situation was draining both my mother and me. We both wanted it over and done with. I was tired of fighting. I had spent the majority of my life fighting and I was just tired.

Ironically, the same night I was rushed to the hospital, my family was already gathered there. My older brother Monroe and his daughter had been in a really bad car accident earlier that evening. I think that night was one of the most upsetting nights my mother had ever experienced. Just imagine she's already upstairs in ICU waiting for one son to come out of surgery when a hospital nurse comes to her and tells her that her youngest son has just been rushed into the emergency room with a head injury. Unbelievable!

Reggie ran from the police for months before they finally caught up with him. He was released on bond before his court date. Reggie already had a criminal record and was no stranger to jail. Reggie managed to track me down shortly after he was released on bond, saying that he just wanted to talk. I gave him five minutes. He pulled out a stack of cash. His proposal was; if I dropped the charges against him, I could have the money. Reggie said that this was all a big misunderstanding that had snowballed. He said that the night he had jumped on me and Greg at the bar was just a case of "wrong place at the wrong time". He blamed his actions on the cocaine that he had been doing that day. I let him know that it wasn't going to happen and he could keep his money. I told him that either he was going to go to jail or one of us was going to end up dead and quite frankly I wasn't ready to die.

Reggie ended up doing about three years for the assault. Right after he was released from jail, he was caught stealing at a super store and stabbed a security guard. He ended up back in jail and that's the last that I've seen or heard of him.

I was still at Avondale Housing when I heard about the maintenance position at Cincinnati Restoration. This was an organization that sponsored housing all over Cincinnati for mental patients. Residents could live independently as long as they took their medications and had some supervision. I applied for and got the job.

My supervisor was a retired gentleman named Henry. Henry and I were the maintenance personnel for all the homes. Maintenance was so unpredictable. No matter how long you are doing it, you always run up against something that you have never done before.

Being around the clients helped me to form a new opinion regarding mental health. I realized how important it was. Clients were from all walks of life. There were clients with Master degrees, Bachelor degrees, black, and white. Some were drug addicts and some simply had a chemical imbalance. Working at CRC taught me that mental illness could destroy anyone's life, including mine. There were times when clients wouldn't take their medications and just lose it. They would walk around without the slightest clue as to what was going on around them. I remember a time when one of the male clients who hadn't taken his medication in some time put his hand in one of the toilets, retrieved some feces and started to consume it. That may sound like a disgusting joke, but mental health is nothing to joke about.

While I was at CRC, my nephew Carlos asked me if I wanted to get an apartment together. I really didn't want to leave my mother, but it was time. I was about twenty-three years old at the time and it was somewhat hard to have a "personal" life living at home with your mother.

The place where Carlos and I moved to was nice. It was a two bedroom with a balcony and outdoor pool. Back then if you had a balcony and pool, you were living all right. Management would let us have late night pool parties. Carlos and I would go out almost every night drinking and partying, but we still got up every morning to handle business. At the time Carlos and I moved in together, I was dating four girls at the same time. There were two girls that I gave the majority of my time to; Dawn and Kathy. One day when Moe was at my house, he saw the picture of Kathy that I had on the television and started to laugh hysterically. Moe had known me for a long time. During that time, he had never known me to be serious with just one girl to act like I was monogamous. Yet, here I was displaying Kathy's picture. Women were an activity for me, nothing to be taken too seriously. You hang out and move on. Besides, before Kathy got pregnant, Moe had never even seen her.

That's right, Kathy got pregnant. When she first told me, I let her know that there was no way she was pregnant by me. She needed to go back and check her facts, get with the real father because it wasn't me. I told her that if she couldn't remember who the father was then she needed to have an abortion because I wasn't taking on the responsibility of another man's baby. Eventually, reality set in. Out of all my other girls, this was the one that I hadn't used protection with. I couldn't grasp the concept that I was her only man. We weren't serious, and she wasn't the only one. This was just the way the game was played.

After I got over the shock of becoming a father, I made up in my mind that I would always be there for my child. Things happen for a reason. I think this was Gods way of showing me just how important it is for a father to have a relationship with his child. Up until that point, I had thought that it wasn't important to have that relationship as long as you had a strong relationship with your mother. Once I fully accepted the fact that Kathy was carrying my child, the bond was instant... even before birth.

Then there was Dawn. Dawn was two months pregnant when I met her so I knew there was no way that I could be that child's father. She was going through the typical drama that most men who are unexpectedly thrust into the role of father would put a woman through. He wanted nothing to do with this baby and I think that's why I became so attached to her. My own father wanted nothing to do with me. For the first time, I could really feel my mother's pain through Dawn.

41

At any rate, Kathy and I had a baby boy. We named him Anthony Lamar Wiley. He was born on the 19th day of January 1987. I was so proud to have that boy. Dawn also had a boy. She named him Jamal, after I convinced her that she shouldn't name him after me. Jamal and I shared a special bond; I knew what he was going to go through. I saw me in him.

Dawn and I had become very close. On Christmas day 1988, she bought me a stuffed Snoopy doll that was about two feet tall, a pair of shoes, an electric blanket and card (Don't laugh, that blanket came in very handy!). When you have two men sharing an apartment, they can be cheap with the household expenses. If we had a choice between money in our pockets or turning the heat up, well… let's just say you'd better keep your coat on when you visit our house.

Anyway, the Christmas card itself was about two feet tall. I knew that Dawn loved me even before the gifts, but she felt like she had to do what she could to hold on to me. She was right; eventually she did lose me. I cared for Dawn and Jamal but I needed to be a father to my son. He needed me.

I returned the gifts to Dawn…except for the blanket and the card. I told her to take the dog and shoes back because she needed the money to take care of Jamal. She told me that was why she loved me so much. She said that she had never met anyone who thought about the well-being of others as much as I did (I know what you're thinking, if I was all that concerned, why didn't I give back the blanket? I told you a brother gets cold during the winter!)

I enjoyed watching Anthony and Jamal grow up and I loved them both. Anthony had a father who spent time with him and cared for him. Jamal didn't. I just couldn't stand thinking about this little boy growing up without a father. It opened up too many old wounds. Eventually I had to choose. Although I would see my son as much as possible, it wasn't enough. I asked Kathy to marry me and she accepted. I never told Dawn that I was going to marry Kathy, but someone else did. I really cared for Dawn and wanted to be with her, but Kathy was the one who had given birth to my son.

So now I was preparing to be Kathy's husband. I knew that I didn't love her, but I wanted to be with my son every day, not just some days. Dawn called me to ask if it were true that I was going to get married. I confirmed that it was true and before I could say anything else, she lashed out and hung up on me. I half understood Dawn's reaction. I understood that she loved me and wanted to be with me, but what I didn't understand was her assumption that I would walk out on my son just as Jamal's father had done. She understood that I knew the pain she was feeling because her son's father wanted nothing to do with him. Yet, she expected me to leave my son for her and Jamal. She expected me to be a part-time father to my son, while being a full-time father to hers.

After Kathy and I married, I found out that Dawn was in the hospital. I was completely stunned to find out that she had tried to end her life. I tried to call her but her family would not let me talk to her. Years went by before I saw Dawn again. I was happy to see that she had moved on with her life. I was even happier to see that she no longer hated me for the choice I had made. As a matter of fact, she said that she now understood and accepted the reason why I got married. She respected me for it. At that time, Kathy and I were divorced.

Our marriage lasted a little over a year. I had married her for the wrong reasons. Kathy and I decided to have a trial separation just to see if what we had was worth salvaging. Kathy and I had been living in the apartment that Carlos and I had shared.

Kathy and I split up in 1989. At that time, I was living in my brother's basement apartment. I began to develop a relationship with a lady named Jasmine and at the same time, I was dating another girl by the name of Kayla. I guess old habits do die hard. Jasmine seemed to be really pro-black. She had just graduated from an all black university and she was really into kids and her community. I admired that because I had become a youth advisor for the Cincinnati Branch NAACP. I was starting to think more about the problems of the black community. I always wondered if I thought about the community problems so much because I was having problems of my own. Although I'm sure that my personal problems had a lot to do with it, I knew that explanation was too simple.

I saw a lot of pain in the faces of blacks and believe it or not, some whites also. Growing up in Lincoln Heights really schooled me on life. Growing up with a strong family unit also prepared me a great deal for life as a man. I realized that my trials and tribulations in life weren't setbacks, but growing pains and learning experiences.

I had taken a job in the mailroom at Chiquita Brands; one of the bigger companies here in Cincinnati. Landing a job in the mailroom wasn't one of my biggest moments in life, but it paid the bills. Needless to say, I wasn't enjoying my job too much. One day after work, a friend and I decided to go out for a couple of drinks. I had just filed bankruptcy and my car was the only thing that I had left. The fact that I had no car insurance didn't keep me from driving. I was driving along on I-75 when a brick wall hit my car (At least that's how I remember it). Our heads went into the windshield. My car was totaled. My friend was all right; He only had a couple of scratches. Meanwhile, the paramedics rushed me to the hospital.

The doctor had to cut off my hair in order to get the glass out of the right side of my head. I had stitches on the right side of my forehead, along the side of my right eye and nose. I spent the day in the hospital. After I was discharged from the hospital, I stayed with my mother for about a month. During that time, you would have thought that I had just had some type of cosmetic procedure. I remember my entire head being wrapped in bandages. I felt like the elephant man. My chest was pretty banged up too. I was truly blessed considering how hard my chest hit the steering wheel. The damage to my chest could have been a lot worse, not to mention that my life had again been spared. By God's grace.

There are consequences for all actions. I was charged with a DUI and had to pay a two hundred and fifty dollar fine. I also had to complete three weekend work details. Could my life have been any worse at this point? Even though my marriage had failed, I had no money, no car, legal troubles, and (potentially) permanent scars from the accident, I felt extremely blessed to still be breathing.

As part of the healing process, I had to go to the hospital regularly for treatment for my face. The doctor was very upfront with me about the long-term outlook on my face healing completely. He said that I would be seriously scarred for the remainder of my life. I was more upset about my face being scarred than I was about any other aspect of my life.

My friend Matt from The Revelation Church of God had become an ordained minister by this time. Sometimes Matt would take me to the hospital for my appointments. One day he asked me if I wanted him to pray for healing. We went to the church and had prayer. Matt said the doctor might say that your face won't heal, but God has told me different. I prayed along with Matt, but my mind really wasn't focused on prayer. My mind was focused on my scarred face. After the prayer was over I looked in the mirror and reality set back in.

My face looked horrible. It didn't look any better after the doctor took the stitches out and the swelling went down. I went from a swollen stitched up face to swollen scars. We all know that the darker the skin, the darker the scars. My right eye was pretty much closed and would stay that way because of the damaged nerves around the eye. Life couldn't get any worse for me. I was just going through the motions. Nothing really meant anything to me. I had lost so much that there was nothing left to lose but myself.

I was really low. I hadn't really dealt with the issues I had as a kid regarding my dark skin and how unattractive it made me feel. How would people treat me now that I was dark and severely scarred? There was nothing appealing about me at all. I was a broke brother, with bad credit, no car, no money, a roach and rat infested apartment and an entry-level mailroom job. I really needed something to hold on to.

I guess God heard my heart. A few months had gone by and I started my day as usual, not really seeing or hearing what was going on around me. I briefly glanced at myself as I walked past a mirror. My eye was completely open and the scars that the doctor said would never heal completely were almost gone. It looked as if the accident had never happened. The doctors had told me that if I didn't have the plastic surgery my face would never be what it used to be. Well God worked his own brand of plastic surgery. I guess this was God's way of letting me know that he was still there. Even though things were at their lowest, God was there. I had something to hold on to now. He is truly a miracle worker!

I had grown tired of working in the mailroom. I was really missing my first love, which was working on homes. I quit my mailroom job and accepted a job working with Community Management. After my three-month license suspension expired, I got another car. The car was older than the one I had previously and it wasn't as nice. However, with the way things were, I was happy I was able to purchase a car at all.

I had always paid Kathy child support. I started paying her on my own the day we split up. After a while she said that it just wasn't enough to take care of Anthony and she needed more. I understood. After sitting down and discussing what she needed, I added an extra twenty dollars to what I was already giving her every two weeks. We both agreed that this would really help. For some reason, I started making my support payments to her by money order instead of cash. I just had this nagging gut feeling I needed to "document" my payments to her. In the meantime, I saw my son faithfully every weekend.

My sisters Roberta and Barbara would get Anthony every chance they got. It was as if my son was their son. Between the two of them, Ant never wanted for anything: clothes, toys, and shoes. A couple of months after Kathy and I had sat down and worked out a new support plan;

I received a court order in the mail. I was furious with Kathy. I called her at work and she agreed to meet with me on her lunch break to discuss why she had done this. Kathy knew that I had always taken care of my son, no matter what was going on in my life. She knew that I always made Ant and his well-being my priority. During our conversation, I asked her what the support order was all about. As I listened to Kathy's words, the rage in my body boiled over. Some people had told her to do it because I would eventually, like all black men, stop caring for and supporting my son.

Kathy knew that I had two motivating forces that would never allow me to turn my back on my son in any way. First and foremost was the love that I felt for my son. This is the same love that made me go against my better judgment and marry a woman that I didn't love. Secondly, my commitment to being a father. Kathy knew that I had never known my father and that I would never do that to my son. She knew how strongly I felt about this. The support order caused more tension between us. As a result, she decided to cut my visitations with my son to no visitation at all.

Kathy lit a fire in me that was unbelievable. This woman had crossed the line. I couldn't do anything about being deprived of a relationship with my own father, but I would not let her take this away from my son and me. That simple piece of paper I received had laid the foundation for our relationship to come. When our court date rolled around, I was still unbelievably angry. The judge pulled out a table they used to determine just how much support non-custodial parents should pay depending on your hourly wage. At the time, I was earning about seven dollars and twenty-five cents. The judge then issued a backorder for well over three thousand dollars!

I got screwed both forward and backward. The judge didn't even want to see the money order receipts that I had kept. The judge said that it was a gift and wasn't considered support. I told the judge that I couldn't afford what I was being asked to pay. I wasn't saying that I wouldn't pay, I was saying that I couldn't afford to pay that amount because I had to take care of myself also. The judges' response? "You had him, you take care of him". I was so angry that I completely forgot about telling the judge that Kathy wouldn't let me see my son.

There was no way this woman was going to take my son away from me. She was not going to come between the two of us. I wasn't going out like that. My mother had always taught me to treat people the way that you want them to treat you. Be upfront and honest with them. Don't run games on anyone because what goes around comes around, but even harder. I had been a fighter all my life and I was more than prepared to fight this woman for my son. That's exactly how I saw her. She was no longer my wife, lover or mother of my child. She was a woman who was more than willing to use my son to tear me apart.

I knew I had to do what had to be done, so I started working a couple side jobs along with my full-time job to support my son. I was working nights and weekends. At that time, Kathy was holding all the cards. I needed to comply as much as possible. If it meant kissing her behind, that was a small price to pay to see my son. Besides, it was only for now. Kathy had started dating someone and I was still dating Jasmine and seeing Kayla occasionally. My brother Clyde and I moved from the apartment in Avondale to a nicer apartment. Things were starting to look up for me. Although I was tired of the drama with Kathy, I was seeing my son on a regular basis.

Clyde let his girlfriend move in with us. I didn't have a problem with it as long as she respected my personal space and me (Besides, it didn't hurt to have someone else contributing). At some point though, Clyde's and my personal items started to come up missing. We didn't pay it much attention at first. We just figured two guys were sharing an apartment, and things were probably being put back in the wrong place. We just figured one had borrowed something from the other and hadn't put it back. It wasn't until we started checking with each other that we realized that a lot of stuff had begun to disappear.

Shortly thereafter, we discovered we had a fourth roommate and his name was "Crack". Clyde's girlfriend had moved her second man into our apartment and she was into him really heavy. I knew it wasn't as simple as just stopping. I had known a lot of friends who were strung out on this drug and it wasn't a joke. My boy Sid still hadn't been able to kick crack. He was in and out of prison for the things he did to support his habit. You name it; he did it. Even though he wasn't willing to admit it at the time, Clyde was fighting a losing battle. I knew what he was going up against and it wasn't going to be easy.

Clyde's girlfriend would disappear for days on end. Then, she would just pop up out of nowhere. One day, on one of her brief visits home, she stole his car and exchanged it for drugs. My brother had to go downtown into one of the most drug-infested areas to get his car back. There was no way I was going to let him go alone. We were both scared to death.

There was no way they were just going to let him have his car back. We would be lucky if they just let us pay what she owed for the drugs. We looked for his car for hours and never did find it. It was probably best that we didn't. I can only imagine what would have happened if we had found his car and the drug dealer that she had traded it to. I don't think he would have just handed the car back over to Clyde along with an apology. Clyde's car and his girlfriend showed back up at the house about three days later. After that, I was gone. It was time for me to move on. I had enough problems in my life without having to deal with theirs.

Kayla had broken up with her boyfriend. They had been dating off and on for about two years. Kayla and I had known each other since we were kids and we dated casually off and on ourselves. It wasn't until a year or so before she and her boyfriend had broken up that we actually got serious and started seeing more of each other. Kayla and I had gone out to a club one night and her ex-boyfriend just happened to be there. Walking through the door I should have known there was going to be some drama. It's bad enough when a girl breaks it off with you, but for her to come walking through the door with some other brother! She's supposed to be at home beating herself up for being so stupid to let you go, or so we like to think. At any rate, I had heard that Kayla's ex-boyfriend had said some bad things about me so I started carrying a knife as a "precaution".

No sooner had we gotten in the door, he approached Kayla and asked her if they could talk. Kayla agreed, figuring if she handles things quietly and pleasantly, he won't make a scene. I should have known his petty behind didn't want anything. I could hear the conversation over the music. This brother actually went "high school" on her. He said that since they were no longer dating, he wanted back everything that he had given her (Now ladies, the worst thing you can do to a man is call him out in public. This is a major "no-no" ladies). Before I knew it, Kayla shouted back to him "Well, give me back the clothes that you have on right now, I'm pretty sure they belong to me". Uh oh, she has set it off now. The argument started. I didn't want to get involved. I had heard that her ex was looking to get me anyway. He didn't appreciate the fact that I had moved in on his girl so quickly. It's no secret that men can be very territorial.

A drunk, jealous brother is not someone that I care to keep company with so I told Kayla that I thought it was time for us to go. Things were escalating between the two of them and I wanted to put some distance between Kayla and her ex. I gently grabbed Kayla's arm and we left the club. Not to my surprise, her ex was following right behind us calling her everything but the "Son of God". Man! I really wasn't looking to have to fight anyone that night, especially him. But I saw it coming. Her ex was about six feet tall and large. He was a weight lifter/wrestler who studied martial arts. Yeah, I was in trouble.

All of a sudden, he picked Kayla up by the neck with both hands and slammed her on the hood of the car. I saw him reaching into his pocket and thought to myself, here we go! As big as this brother was he felt as if he needed a pair of brass knuckles to whoop my tail. Kayla no longer was the focus of his rage. Now it was my turn. He looked at me and told me that he had wanted me for some time now (If you've learned anything from me while reading you know that I never run from anyone). Now I had done the bigger thing by leaving the club, and I had also done the bigger thing by ignoring his words of disrespect. I was not about to let this man chase me down and beat me down.

He and I were exchanging blows for what seemed to be a good twenty minutes. In actuality, it was only a brief couple of minutes. It doesn't take long for those knuckles to wear you down. I couldn't take much more of them; he and those knuckles were beating me into the ground. This man was going to try and beat me to death. I did the only thing I could. I reached in my pocket and pulled out the knife. Stabbing him was the last thing I wanted to do. However, there was no way he was going to let me walk away. He was going to beat me until I didn't get back up.

After I pulled the blade out of him, he dropped to his knees. I'll never forget the look of disbelief on his face, and I'll never forget the sickening fear that I felt. He stumbled to his car and drove off. Fist fighting was one thing, but my actions in that one split second had the potential to take this man's life. Even though I felt that my life was in danger, I never intended to take his. I was just defending myself. This was not something that I wanted. I never thought that I would actually be a part of the black-on-black crime stats that white reporters rattle off every evening on the 6:00 o'clock news.

I left the club parking lot knowing that there was nothing within my power that I could do to make this right. I had left the club and walked away from him, but he still followed. Even though my actions were clearly self-defense, my heart was heavy. I couldn't believe what I had done. Why does trouble always find me? I was extremely upset with myself. Trying to convince myself that it was either him or me didn't make me feel any better. If anything, it made me feel worse. The thought that he would willingly take my life over something stupid upset me even more. For all I knew, he could have been somewhere dead. I may have actually taken someone's life.

Kayla was living with her parents at the time so I took her home. I then went home myself. That night seemed to be one of the longest nights of my life. Needless to say, I didn't sleep the whole night. I just lay there asking myself over and over how? How could I take another person's life? That wasn't my way of thinking. That wasn't the way my mother raised me. With all I saw in my younger days, the drugs, the violence, and death; I wanted to be a part of the solution, not a part of the problem.

I called my brother Monroe and told him what had happened. He came over to the house. He could see just how hard I was taking what had happened. He assured me that everything would work out. He said that he knew I wasn't a bad person and that I didn't intend to do Kayla's ex any harm. Monroe just reassured me of what I had already known. We all know who and what we are at heart. Since the day I caught the picture of Jesus in my hands, I've known that God was watching over me. The stabbing incident forced me to look at all the other incidents that had happened in my life and what had led up to them.

Even though my life was plagued with such drama, not once did I ever think about giving up on life or myself. I still had the desire to help make this world a better place. I've had friends that have given up on life and many of them are no longer with us. Sid was my first and best friend. In his late teens, whenever we talked, he would just tell me how tired he was. At the time I didn't understand exactly what he meant. I wasn't sure how to respond so I usually said nothing. I wasn't sure if it was God pushing me or if I was just hard headed. I wasn't a quitter and my desire to help rebuild our community grew even stronger as I grew stronger. The one thing that I did know was that God would reveal to me just what my purpose was and why I had gone through so much.

The next day Kayla called me. Her ex was in the hospital in critical condition. It was hard to make out what she was saying through the tears, but I understood enough to know that he might die. I was speechless. My whole life, gone in an instant. There was a very good chance that I wouldn't get to do all the good things I wanted to do. There was a good chance that I would be spending a lot of time in prison. I asked Kayla to continue to keep me informed on his condition and she said she would. Before Kayla hung up the phone, she also let me know that his sister had taken out a warrant for my arrest.

The next day I went to visit my mom in Lincoln Heights. While we were sitting on the porch, a Lincoln Heights police cruiser drove down the street. He stopped and came back to talk to me. Fortunately for me, the officer in the cruiser was someone I had grown up with. He called me over to the car and asked me if I knew about the warrant. I admitted that I did and told him I appreciated him not saying anything in front of my mother. As he began to ask me questions, I told him the entire story. He advised me to turn myself in. He also told me that I should file a warrant against Kayla's ex.

I wasted no time. I went to Lincoln Heights Police Station where they kept me in a holding cell until I could be transported to the Hamilton County Justice Center in downtown Cincinnati. I sat in that cell for two hours. It was the longest two hours of my life. I got a glimpse of what my life would be like for the next ten years or so. Sitting in a cell with someone dictating your every move.

When it was time to transport me to the justice center, the cop who drove me down just put me in the back seat of the cruiser. He didn't bother with handcuffs because he and I had also grown up together. I knew almost every officer on the force. The drive to the justice center was humiliating and shameful. What would Kathy tell my son?

What would my mother think? What would my brothers and sisters think of me now? No matter what, they would always love me, but would they see me differently? Would they be disappointed in me?

When we finally arrived at the justice center, I was told to put my hands behind my back as I got out of the cruiser. He told me that even though he didn't want to use the cuffs, he had to do his job. He couldn't just let me walk into the justice center unrestrained. It was at that instance that I realized that I was a prisoner and had to be treated as such. The officers at Lincoln Heights Police Department treated me as a friend because that's how they viewed me. Hamilton County treated me as a criminal. And by legal standards, I was.

I let him know that it was all right, that I expected him to do his job. I thanked him for his kindness and told him that I knew exactly how he felt when he put me in the cruiser with no cuffs on. I thanked him for his love and support.

I was searched, fingerprinted and locked in a cell with about twenty other guys. Best case: assault. Worst case: murder. Either way, I was going to do time. I was scared to death. I had never been in jail before. Images of crazy Danny Racker and the butt whipping he had put on me all those years ago flooded my head. Even though they were two totally different incidents with completely different outcomes, the fear I felt each time was exactly the same. Through the years I had never felt the same intensity of fear that I felt the day Danny jumped out of the bushes on me. That is, never until today.

As I sat quietly, the other guys were asking each other what they were in for. Most of the guys were proud of their actions and didn't seem to have a care in the world. I knew then that jail wasn't for me. I was going to fight like never before to make sure that I didn't have to spend any more time in here.

Four hours later, my mother and sister Shirley came to bail me out. My sister had to put up the bond because my mother didn't have it. Even though I had never been in jail and didn't have a criminal record, the judge wouldn't let me out on my own recognizance. My sister had to put down five hundred dollars before I could walk out of there.

Kayla's ex was still in the hospital. The first thing I did after leaving the justice center was to take my friends advice and file a warrant on him. He was released from the hospital about a month later, an entire month. I never imagined that I did so much damage. It just let's you know just how fragile the human body really is.

My mother recommended a good lawyer. Our court date was approaching and she wanted to make sure that the attorney and I were more than prepared to pull together a credible case. We had been to court a couple of times and Kayla's ex wasn't letting up. Neither was I. Kayla came to me and told me that she had started dating her ex again. I was furious. Here I am getting ready to go to jail over some dumb mess. Kayla was getting ready to start keeping house with the man who had gotten me into this mess! Had she forgotten just how hard of a beating I had taken at the hands of this man? Had she forgotten that if it weren't for the knife I would have most likely died in that parking lot? Before I could fire back at her, Kayla said that she started dating him again because it was the only way she could get him to drop the charges against me. I couldn't let her do that. I knew what this man was capable of. I watched him pick her up by the throat and toss her onto the hood of a car that night. I knew he wouldn't think twice about hurting her again.

I told her thanks, but there's no need to start dating him on my account. Her mind was already made up. Nothing I said or did was going to change it. I knew she felt responsible for what was happening and she didn't want me to go to jail for defending myself. She also knew that her ex was only pursuing the charges because he was jealous. He figured that if I was in jail, we couldn't see each other.

At our next court date, his attorney came over to our table and told us that his client was going to drop the charges and asked if I was willing to do the same. We both agreed to drop the charges and walked out of the courtroom as free men.

I felt so badly for Kayla. She had given up her freedom so that I could keep mine. This woman had been trying so hard for the longest time to break it off with him. He harassed and stalked this woman for the better part of a year. I remember hearing the fear in her voice when she talked about him. She couldn't get away from him. She finally got away only to be forced back.

Kayla's actions weren't surprising. I knew the type of person she was and there was no way she was going to let me go to jail for protecting myself. She knew that it was her ex who was at fault, but she also knew that he would never be a man and own up to it. She felt it was her responsibility to make it right since he would not. I just wanted to put this part of my life far behind me and move forward. It was time for me to move forward with my life.

"We have made such great strides over the years. There are so many successful African-Americans all around us for a people who started out with nothing but hope."

Chapter 5

Realizing What Life Is About

I moved into a third floor, one bedroom apartment in May 1990. My apartment wasn't the best looking, but it was nice. I had bought another car and a truck for work. It really felt like the fog that had engulfed my life for so long, was finally lifting. I had only been in my new apartment for about three months when a partner of mine asked me if he could stay with me. I was really looking forward to having my own space and wasn't much feeling like a roommate, but I figured I would return the favor that my brother had done for me. I agreed to allow my friend to stay, but I made it clear to him that it was only temporary.

One of my other partners, Toney, had recently relocated to Atlanta, so the time seemed right for a well-deserved vacation. I contacted my "temporary" roommate, my nephew Carlos and Perry, who was another friend of mine, and we all decided to take a road trip to Atlanta. I remember how fly we felt riding in those rented '89 Dodge Dynasties! One was white and the other was blue. You couldn't tell us that we weren't rollin'!

We arrived on a Thursday night. We stayed in adjoining suites in a downtown hotel right on the famous "Peachtree" Street. Carlos had family in Atlanta. When they heard we were in town, they came over to our suite along with Toney. We all hung out and kicked it the entire weekend. Man, I sure needed this weekend. When I think back on all that was going on in my life at that time, I'm surprised my head just didn't explode. We had an excellent time. I remember thinking to myself; "this is what life is about". And money wasn't an issue. We all had plenty of it to throw around so we spent the entire weekend living large!

Sunday morning had arrived way too quickly, but it was time to get back on the road. With much hesitation, we loaded up the cars and headed back to Cincinnati. We weren't even an hour and a half outside of Atlanta when we noticed a plain black police vehicle following us. Every time we would change lanes, so would he. This went on for about sixty miles or so. Finally, the unmarked car pulled us over. Shortly thereafter, five other police vehicles arrived. This being my first trip so far away from home, I wasn't sure exactly what was happening or why. The officer asked Carlos and me to get out of the car and he asked for identification from both of us. Since I was driving, I gave him my license. He told us that they had received a call about someone transporting drugs across the state and that the suspects were believed to be traveling in new model Dynasties. The officer then asked us to get out of the car so that they could conduct a search. I glanced in my side view mirror and saw that the other officers were detaining Perry and my roommate. Carlos and I got out of the car. I don't know what came over him, but when Carlos got out of the car, he continued to walk toward the woods and away from the car. One of the officers yelled for him to stop and drew his gun out of the holster. I yelled for Carlos to stop. I asked him if he was crazy or just ready to die! Carlos said that he didn't realize that we had to stay there while they were searching.

He just had to go to the bathroom. The officer angrily told Carlos that he should never walk away when an officer has stopped him.

We told the officers that we didn't do drugs nor did we have any in the car (At this point in my life, the call for weed was long gone.). There was no need for them to search our vehicle. The officer let us know that we had two choices. We could either give them permission to search the car or we could be detained while they obtained a search warrant for the cars. If we chose the latter of the two, we would most likely be waiting on the side of the road for a couple of hours. Considering the fact that it was winter and freezing outside, we did not want to spend the next two hours or so standing outside in the elements. We were hesitant, but we gave them permission to search our cars. Besides, we knew that they weren't going to find anything, because there was nothing to find.

After searching both cars and coming up empty, they released all four of us. We drove on until we came to a gas station where we could stop and compose ourselves. Perry was very upset, a little more upset than what he should have been. I asked him what had happened with the police but he wouldn't say. Perry was a shaking mess. He had tears in his eyes. My roommate explained that when the police pulled them over, they asked Perry for his license. Perry hadn't told us that he didn't have a license. When Perry couldn't produce a license, the officer pulled his firearm on Perry, pointed it straight at his head and yelled "Nigger, get out of the car"! It wasn't until that moment that we realized that there was no anonymous call regarding the possibility of drugs being transported through Atlanta. Those cops had just profiled us. We hadn't had a clue. They took one look at us; our out of state plates and came to the conclusion that we were dangerous, gun-toting drug dealers. Reality had just slammed our well-deserved getaway. Was it too much to ask to be able to get away from the craziness for just one weekend? "To be a black man in America" was often a phrase I heard, but never quite understood. I sure did understand it now. I couldn't catch a break within my own community. Now it looked like I wasn't going to catch one outside either. What do you do when you feel like you have nowhere to go?

My roommate stayed with me for about eight months. Even though we had a good time, I was more than ready for him to go. In the meantime, I had heard about a national property management company named Fath Management that had some of the best apartment complexes in the city. This was one of the largest property management companies in the greater Cincinnati area. They were looking for maintenance personnel. I applied for the position and was asked to take a written test and drug test, all before I got an interview. After two interviews, they finally offered me the job in Occupied Service. When I started the job in September my supervisor was a white female. She and I were the only two who ran occupied tickets. Her boss was also in the vacant apartments department. My starting pay wasn't great, but I knew there was room for advancement so I stuck it out.

I worked under her supervision for about a year and did excellent work. She would always tell me that I was very good at what I did. She later accepted a job with another company and another guy in the Vacant Services area became my supervisor. Another maintenance person was hired to replace him.

At that time, things were going swell. I had a good job and a nice apartment. Best of all, I had just met a young lady named Tracey. She was dealing with some challenges of her own and initially just needed a friend. We were spending so much time together and we realized that feelings had developed on both sides. Imagine how excited I was when she agreed to move in with me! We lived in my apartment for a short time before we moved into a much nicer townhouse owned by the property management company I worked for. It was nice... real nice. It had a fireplace, patio and two bedrooms. The fact that I received a discount on the rent made it even sweeter.

In January of 1993, some friends of mine and I were making plans to travel back to Atlanta to celebrate Dr. Martin Luther King Jr.'s birthday. That's right, we were going back! We made plans to leave on the 16th of January, which was a Friday. The day before we were to leave, we all decided to go to a well-known neighborhood bar in Lincoln Heights. Moe, Carlos, Ellic, Stone, Danny Cook, my old roommate and I were having a good time drinking and partying. I decided to play a quick game of pool. Since there was no wait, I asked one of my boys if he wanted to join me. Even though there was no one playing pool at the time, there were a bunch of guys leaning on the table. We walked over to the table and I asked the group of guys "who's got next?" No one answered me so I put my money on the table and started to rack the balls. Just as my friend was getting ready to break, some guy (who was all of six feet four inches tall) rushed over to the table, picked up the ball and proceeded to clear the table.

This brother started yelling all kinds of obscenities at my partner and me. He said I told you no one was allowed to play pool. I turned to my boy and said, "I must have missed something, who is this?" He looked at me and said, "who are you?" My response to the man's question was to ask him a question in the form of "who are you? At that moment, someone touched my arm and said "Chuck, can I talk to you for a moment". It was an old friend that I had grown up with. He told me that the guy who was trying to "house" the pool table was a dope dealer. I realized then that the group of guys leaning on the pool table before were nothing but a bunch of dope boys. I knew all of these guys. They were from zone 15, and I had grown up with some of them.

The big upset brother then introduced himself and proceeded to recite his lineage to me. His name was Benny and he had just done ten years for murder. I then told him that my name was Charles and I didn't care how many years he had done or what he had done them for. This was zone 15 and he wasn't running anything here! How are these dealers from zone 15 going to let someone outside the zone come in and shut down the pool table? I was pissed. At this point, some of the people at the bar were trying to keep Benny and me apart. A crowd had gathered and most of my boys were in the crowd, not knowing that I was in the center of the chaos. Joe and Gil, who I also grew up with, were also in the bar that night. My boy was still holding the pool rack trying to get to me. Any insult he could think of came flying out of his big mouth.

Carlos pulled me away and told me to stay cool. He reminded me that we were about to go to Atlanta and we didn't need this right now. I knew he was right. I looked at Benny and he was now throwing his insults at Gil. Gil and Benny must have known each other because Benny was asking Gil what he had to do with it. Gil let him know that he and I were like brothers. Benny now focused his attentions and hostility on Gil. By that time, I had heard enough of this idiot's mouth and wanted to shut him up. There was just something about dope boys that set me off. They just felt like they ran everything and everyone. Like everyone should bow down to them or something. I couldn't take it any longer. I hit Benny dead center in the side of his face. Blood was pouring from his mouth as he hit the floor. His brother Jake, who was also in the bar that night and who was also from zone 15, started fighting with Carlos. Before you knew it, it was us against the dope boys. Tables and chairs were flying; bottles and glasses were being smashed. One of the guys that was with Benny was preparing to blow the back of my head off when Gil ran over and grabbed him. I didn't know the guy, but Gil did. Instead of shooting me, the guy ran out the back door and fired in the air. The fight was over. Police were coming from everywhere and people were running to get away. However, I wasn't leaving until I found the gold watch and necklace that my baby Tracey had just bought me for my 30th birthday.

We left for Atlanta the next day, as if nothing had happened (The only evidence was the fact that my boy Moe had to ride the whole way with a steak over his eye). I was particularly quiet the entire way down. I don't know if it was the realization of that gun being pointed at the back of my head and the guy holding it a split second away from pulling the trigger or just what. What if Gil hadn't caught him? All I knew was that I was tired of all of this. I had had enough of the violence. It didn't matter who was to blame or who the innocent bystanders were. Between the drugs and violence, I felt as if the black community was literally being destroyed.

While in Atlanta, I had the honor of meeting the wife of Dr. Martin Luther King Jr. It was truly a privilege and honor to have the pleasure of meeting Coretta Scott King. Black History had always meant so much to me. I would sometimes try to imagine what it was like being on the front lines of the civil rights war. I could only imagine what they had gone through. I would oftentimes find myself thinking about our ancestors being torn away from their families and homeland. Brought to this new world not as people, but as property to be used and abused. I often tried to imagine what it must have been like to live life as a slave, never really being in complete control of ones own life. I tried to imagine how they felt having their families torn apart by separation because the slave owner could no longer afford to feed all the slaves. Either that or a slave owner may have felt the offer made by another white man to purchase one of his slaves was just too good to pass over. The truth is, I just couldn't come close to what they were feeling. Reminding myself of what my ancestors had endured kept me from feeling sorry for myself simply because my life wasn't perfect. When I read and heard about some of the things they were made to endure, it made my trials seem meaningless.

Being in Atlanta celebrating Dr. King's birthday made me think of these things even more. I tried to put myself in the shoes of some of our great leaders: Fredrick Douglas, Harriett Tubman, Marcus Garvey, Malcolm X and the great Dr. King Jr. No matter how hard I tried to put myself in their place, my mind just wouldn't take me there. However, those three days in Atlanta helped me to wake up. Those three days helped me to see what I had been missing all these years. It helped me to see that I was guilty of treating our black communities the same way that people treated me as a child because of my dark skin. I was treating our black communities like a dark-skinned child. Instead of seeing all the darkness in the black communities, I was now able to see the beauty and strength within our communities.

As a people, we have been enslaved for over 250 years. Now we were enslaving ourselves. Drugs and violence were controlling our black communities. Drugs and violence were controlling us, as individuals and as a community. We have spent the last 150 years trying to rebuild the black family and our black communities; however, at the same time, we have spent the last 150 years tearing them apart along with outside influences.

We have made such great strides over the years. There are so many successful African-Americans all around us. For a people who started out with nothing but hope, it's absolutely amazing. That just goes to show what can be done when we come together. We are doctors, lawyers, business owners, professors, architects, artists, politicians, writers, blue collar and white collar. My second trip, to Atlanta, was truly life changing.

"Black Positive Brothers (BPB) was an organization established to help educate and enhance African-American communities."

Chapter 6

The Positive Outweighs the Negative

The weekend after the trip to Atlanta, I called and contacted six of my close friends and asked them to meet at my house for an important discussion. It was held on the 2nd weekend of February 1993. I knew that the time was right for what I had planned. In attendance were Greg Smith, Dell King, Moe Givens, Carlos Jones, Kevin Jones, his brother and Danny Parker.

I had told them very little about my reasons for wanting to meet with them. I had given them just enough to peak their interest and make sure that they showed up for the meeting. The day of the meeting, we all sat down at my kitchen table and I shared my ideas on starting an organization to help deal with some of the problems plaguing our communities. That month, in February 1993, Black Positive Brothers was formed.

Black Positive Brothers, or BPB, was an organization established to help educate and enhance African-American communities. We formed a board consisting of all those who were in attendance that day. Carlos, President; Moe, Vice President; Kevin, Treasurer; Dell, Danny and Greg were board members. I rounded things out by taking on the position of CEO. This small, cohesive group of members was more than willing to do what had to be done to help the cause. Before we could get anything done, we had to come up with some funds. We all came out of our pockets with $150 to $200 each. It wasn't a lot, but it would help get things started.

For uniforms, we decided on black berets with a patch in the shape of Africa encircled in an outline of gold and black on the front of the hat. Each member was to wear a nice suit and tie along with the berets. The berets were our sign of strength. The continent of Africa represented our ancestry. The circle around the continent meant unity. Our colors were black and gold: the gold symbolized the riches of the African land and the kings and queens of whom we were descendents. Of course I prayed to God before I called for the meeting, as I did everything.

We decided to throw a party to introduce ourselves to the community and to raise some desperately needed funds. The party was packed! Everyone loved our ideas and the unity we represented. Later that summer, we hosted a cookout at the park, which included free food, games for the kids and information on drugs in our communities and black-on-black violence. The support from the community was growing. My family, which is pretty large in size, was definitely in our corner.

BPB didn't have a formal office but ran very efficiently out of our home. Tracey and my niece were very supportive in doing secretarial work for us. Our home phone was starting to ring constantly. People were calling wanting to find out more about the organization and men were calling wanting to know about membership. Additionally, strangers and people in the general public were calling to find out when and where our next function was going to take place.

The organization was developing a huge following. The word was out.

At the time, membership was closed. We had so much going on and such a small group of people doing the work that we couldn't take on an active membership drive. I was very excited and proud of what we were doing. Additionally, I was amazed at just how fast the organization had taken off. One of our first priorities was our mentoring program. We were pairing at-risk, troubled kids with mentors. For the first time, I finally saw a purpose for my life. I finally started to understand that things really do happen for a reason. I had founded an organization and was actively running it! It had the potential to do so much good, I had a wonderful woman in my life that was strong and believed in me, and I had a job, which I loved to show up for every morning. Furthermore, my relationship with my son was stronger than ever.

Unfortunately, the relationship between my son's mom and I was a totally different story. Things between the two of us were still about the same. Nothing had changed. It was somewhat ironic. I was good at bridging the gaps within our communities, but I still hadn't found a way to bridge the gap between Kathy and me. There was some extra icing on the cake. I was about to start what I thought of as my dream job.

After years of working in my chosen field, I finally found a company I enjoyed working for. The name of the company was Fath Management. At the time I didn't know it, but I would soon grow to regret ever hearing that name. What Fath Management did to me nearly destroyed my wife's and my life. Their philosophy seemed to be: "If you're white, your right. If you're black, get back".

At the time, I was the only African-American working on one of the larger properties owned by Fath Management. This made it somewhat hard for the white guys who worked in HVAC and Maintenance to share black and Jewish jokes. This was the only part of my job that I didn't enjoy: the ignorant crewmembers. In the past, I probably would have gotten upset and boxed someone's head. However, with age, I had learned to overlook a lot of things that I normally wouldn't have. Besides, I was tired of the "negative" fight; I wanted to focus all my energy on the "positive" fight.

The property was about 1800 units. I also worked at two smaller properties, both properties having a combined total of somewhere around 350 units. Between the three complexes, I would say that at least 80% of the tenants were black.

I was working very hard doing my share and sometimes my co-workers' share of the work. My work was frequently referred to as excellent and the word was getting around. On one particular property, we had a problem with electrical shortages. This was due to the fact that some parts of the complex had copper wiring and other parts had aluminum wiring. Man, I was quick! I could fix just about anything and when it came to troubleshooting, there was none other like me. I knew I was good, but I never advertised it. Bragging and boasting about how good you are isn't exactly the right path for the only brother at the company to take. However, my manager at the time started to take notice. Out of nowhere, I started seeing more faces that looked like mine. I guess he figured since I was doing the work of two men, six could do the work of twelve. He even hired a black, female leasing agent. Word had it that they were so impressed with my work that they decided to take a chance and hire more blacks. I remember when one of the guys actually told me that during the entire time he had been employed with the company, he had never seen a black person working in maintenance, or any other department... until I was hired. In some ways, I guess I had proved the old stereotype about blacks being lazy to be wrong.

Shortly after the new workers were hired, my supervisor gave his notice and left the company. The manager, Jimmy called me into the office, where I was informed that a lot of changes were going to be made. I was told that the owner of the company wanted the property to be brought up to 110% in every area. This included the outside appearance, the appearance of the apartments, maintenance, etc. At the time, there were nearly 300 empty apartments that needed to be prepared for move-in. At the same time, there were over 100 work orders for maintenance in the occupied apartments. Jimmy told me that they were going to combine the vacant crew, occupied crew and new hires into one team. I was told that they had been watching me and that I had more than proved myself capable of the job. I wasn't aware of any job openings. To my knowledge, there wasn't one. I was also told that since they were combining all the crews together that the vacant supervisor was being promoted to property manager and they needed someone to supervise the entire maintenance personnel. This had never been done before and they were offering me the job. Ah yeah, there's going to be a party in the big house tonight! I couldn't believe it. I knew that I was deserving of the job. I just never imagined that a company who had never hired a black employee would offer me a supervisor position.

As part of my new role, I would be supervising the vacant crew, occupied crew, housekeepers, grounds men, purchasing, subcontracting, carpet cleaners and installers. Jimmy wanted me to take the job because he knew that I could handle it. He also wanted me to be clear on just how much responsibility I would be taking on (Did I forget to mention the nice pay increase that came with it?). I let him know that I appreciated his confidence in me and that I was honored that I was being asked to take on such a responsibility. I let him know that I needed some time to think things over and get back to him. Even though I was really excited about the new job offer and was about 60% sure I would be accepting the job, I wanted to talk things over with Tracey. I wanted to be sure that I could handle the job. It was going to be a tedious and tiresome uphill battle. Remember the company's goal: they wanted the property at 110%.

Three days had passed before I officially accepted the job. My boss was very happy that I accepted. He really did believe in me. His extending the offer to me wasn't something that he had taken lightly. He had given it some considerable thought. If he had any doubts as to my ability to do the job and be successful at it, he would have never even considered me for the position. Jimmy had been checking out my work long enough to know exactly what he was doing and what he was getting.

"We must never give up!"

Chapter 7

Discrimination Almost Destroyed My Life

On the day I started my new position at Fath, I was called into a meeting with all of the employees that were going to be reporting to me. A few other key members of the team were also in attendance. My promotion was formally announced along with the new way things would be operating. For the most part, everyone seemed to be happy that I was the new supervisor. Along with supervising the maintenance, housekeeping and ground personnel, I would also be working closely with the leasing agents. Dealing with the leasing agents directly was the most efficient way to monitor the comings and goings in the complex. I had been around for a few years so I knew how things worked. If I wanted things to change for the better, I would have to come up with a new system. After Jimmy left the meeting, I took over and explained a few of the changes that I had in mind. In the beginning, it was business as usual. You can't throw too much change at people too quickly.

The one change I initiated right off was to have everyone pick up his daily work assignments each morning when they arrived and drop them off each evening before leaving the job. This way, I kept track of what had gotten done each day and what still needed to be done. It also let me know who needed help and in what area. The team knew that if they weren't able to fix or clean something that they should move on to the next work order and radio me to let me know about the problem. It was then my responsibility to take the time to train that individual to make the repair. This way the next time, and there would be a next time; they would be able to handle it on their own. Before I had become the supervisor, I had witnessed some workers take up to four hours on a repair that should have only taken them about thirty minutes. Of course, that's if they had been trained properly in the beginning. I also did my part to make sure that I pulled us together as a team. If one of my maintenance personnel was behind on a repair and we were working on borrowed time, I had no problem assisting. My motto: Anything to get the job done, right and on time. Just like BPB, I took pride in my job and loved it.

The way I had pulled all of us together as a team did wonders for the workers' morale and the environment. They were now at ease. They were working very hard and enjoying their work. I was getting the most out of them without overworking them. We were productive and my organization was really starting to take flight.

Meanwhile, the BPB Executive board had decided to open membership to the community. Men were coming from everywhere to become members of Black Positive Brothers. I had a lot on my plate at the time, but my life was really going well. I honestly thought that all the drama I had dealt with in my younger days was behind me for good and that it was now time for me to reap the benefits of my hard work. I decided to ask my longtime girlfriend Tracey to marry me. The fact that she said yes was yet another indication of how good life was. I felt blessed in a lot of ways.

My workday started an hour before my workers were due in. Every Tuesday morning I checked inventory and supplies. I had to make sure that we had everything we needed on hand to get the job done. We didn't have the luxury of being able to wait around for a part to come in. It had to be "demand on hand". At least twice a week I checked vacant apartments to see what was needed. This was the first time during my tenure with the company that I had seen all three properties caught up and doing so well. Within six months, my crew and I had completely turned things around. Needless to say, Jimmy was very happy with me.

Things were going really well but there was one thing missing: the pay increase. I had been doing this job for the past six months and I hadn't yet received the pay increase that I was promised. On five separate occasions, I had asked Jimmy when I was going to receive my pay increase for the job. He would always say that it was coming. Needless to say, it never did.

Finally Jimmy called me in and I received my first evaluation as a supervisor. The evaluation was okay, but nothing like when he would just stop me in passing to tell me what an outstanding job I was doing. During my evaluation, he also let me know that he had hired a second supervisor. The new supervisor would be taking over **half of my responsibilities.** He said that he realized that my job was too much for one person even though I had been doing a good job. I began to get a nasty feeling in the pit of my stomach. If that wasn't enough, that scheming back-stabber only gave me a **.25-cent raise!**

"Upset" couldn't begin to explain how I felt. I voiced my disagreements with him about his decision to hire a second supervisor and the embarrassing raise he had given me. I don't know why I wasted my breath because he didn't hear a word that I said. Jimmy came into that office with his mind already made up. In fact, his mind was made up six months ago when he offered me the job. It was staring me right in the face. They had no intentions on letting me keep that position. They were only going to let me keep the position long enough to get things caught up and get the properties in tip top shape. That was the plan from the very beginning. That explains the poor evaluation that he had given me. Now that the properties were up to speed and running smoothly, they planned to slowly squeeze me out by making it look as if I couldn't handle the job. They didn't want to highlight anything major because it would contradict everything they had been telling me over the past six months. They would start small and slow. To start, a forgotten work order here or there.

I knew what was coming. And I would have bet money that the man he had hired was white. I guess they figured that the predominately black crew would be more likely to work harder and get the job done if it were one of their own giving the orders. He knew what the plan was from jump. Thinking proactively, I started keeping notes and every document I could get my hands on. I kept company newsletters telling everyone about my promotion to supervisor, vacation forms that I had signed for my crewmembers, and any form that I was given as a supervisor. I made copies of everything. Just when I thought things couldn't possibly get much worse, that idiot expected me to train the second supervisor. Isn't this about nothin! You take half my job from me because you say it's too much work for one person, but you go and hire someone who has no experience or skills at all. He may not have had skills, but he had the right color.

The new supervisor's name was Dan. I trained him for about a month. I showed him where to go on the properties and what to do, but he couldn't fix anything. At the end of that month, he took over the vacant apartments, housekeeping and contractors. I was left with occupied, inventory and supplies. At the time, I hadn't been wearing a uniform because once you were a supervisor; you could wear your street clothes, provided they were nice and professional. One day Dan and I were outside talking when the property manager Jeff approached us. He walked up to me and told me to start wearing my uniform again. He didn't ask me if I would: he just told me to do it. Of course, I questioned him. Dan wasn't required to wear a uniform, so why did I have to start wearing a uniform again? By this time, Dan had interrupted and stated that he would like to continue wearing his clothes and that he didn't want to wear a uniform. Jeff said to him, "I wasn't talking to you, I was talking to Charles". I knew exactly what they were doing. They didn't want to come out and tell me that they were putting me back in maintenance and that Dan was now the only supervisor. The cowards were afraid that if they did that, the work wouldn't get done anymore. So, they figured that if they let it look like the nigger was still in charge, then the other niggers would continue to perform.

I could see the writing on the wall and so could most of my crew. I became very quiet and withdrawn at work and things just kept getting worse. One day while I was entering the office, I overheard a conversation between Dan and Jeff. Jeff told Dan that even though he was on salary wages, he still had to fill out a time sheet. While they were out taking "101 Ways to Screw a Black man over for His Job and Get Away with it", they should have been taking "Whispering

101" because I heard every word they said. I felt like throwing up. Even with the .25-cent raise I had received, I was still only making about $9.00 an hour. I knew for a fact that if you were a salaried employee, you were making no less than $12.00 an hour. Dan was getting paid $3.00 more than I for doing only half the job that I was doing. At work, I felt like a nobody. I was embarrassed and humiliated. Before this, I didn't really know what depression was.

On the other hand, BPB was doing really well. It was the one thing that made me feel worthy. My family and friends tried to understand what I was going through, but they just didn't get it. I was living with my work situation everyday, and everyday it got worse. They were all supportive and helpful, but I was in it alone.

BPB made me feel good. People depended on me; our communities were starting to look up to the organization. I never really let my family know just how deeply I was hurting. I had been this way since I was a child. Maybe I didn't let them know because I didn't know how to express what I was feeling in a way that they would understand.

A few months after everything had started, Jimmy resigned and a woman named Betty took his place. In June 1994, she called me into her office and said that she wanted me to go back into the maintenance department because I was a hard worker and I could get a lot more done in maintenance. I refused. I informed her that I wanted to exercise my seniority rights and that she should put Dan into maintenance. I had worked too hard and too long for them to do this to me. This can't be happening. The previous Manager didn't have the balls to do it himself, so he took the cowardly way out of it. They left it for the new Manager to handle.

The look on her face and the next words out of her mouth sealed everything up for me. She looked in my file and she said to me, **"I don't know what kind of games this company has been playing with you, but you are not in the files as a supervisor"**. I lost it, right then and there. I felt like my head was going to explode. I was beyond upset! I was shaking and nervous; by now the tears were rolling down my face. Never had I felt hate at that level before. I had trusted Jimmy and the rest of the company. I thought he was a cool person. I really thought that he meant what he said. But why? If they didn't want me to have the job, why give it to me? I didn't ask for the job: they came to me and offered it. Jimmy had screwed me over big time and didn't lose one night sleep while doing it. How can you screw around with someone's life so badly and not feel a thing? I asked if I could go home sick. I told her how I was feeling and she agreed that I should take the day off.

The next day I went to see my family doctor about a really bad headache I had. It had been bothering me since my conversation with Betty and didn't seem to be letting up any. I told my doctor what I felt was the reason for the headaches. I also told him that I was worried because they didn't seem to be getting any better. They seemed to be getting worse. My doctor recommended a psychologist by the name of John Thomas. Now I know most people would be somewhat ashamed of having to see a psychologist, but I wasn't. I realized that there was something very much wrong with me and I wanted to get better. I just didn't know how. My thoughts often went back to my days when I was working for Cincinnati Restoration. It was if God had prepared me for this. If I would not have worked at Cincinnati Restoration and seen the seriousness of mental health, I would have never known that I had developed a mental illness stemming from my job situation. I had witnessed mental illness ravage the lives of some of the most ordinary people. My emotional state scared me to death. I was so afraid that I was losing my mind. My emotions and mental state were out of control and I had no idea how to regain that control.

My mental state was so bad at that time that Dr. Thomas took me off work immediately. It was my first visit and he made it clear to me that it would be in my best interest not to return to work until he had released me. Dr. Thomas said that I was suffering significant depression, anxiety and stress, all related to my current job situation. During one of my sessions with Dr. Thomas, I had the opportunity to tell him about my newly formed organization. He liked the idea and was very impressed. He insisted that I continue my work with BPB because it was something that the community needed and he said that it would also serve as a form of therapy for me. It would help me to rebuild my confidence and self-esteem. I couldn't believe it. I had gone through so much pain while growing up and never had I lost my pride or self-esteem. Fath had taken it all in less than seven months. I would visit with Dr. Thomas at least twice a month. Even though I was hurting on the inside and some days I felt dead, I had to do everything I possibly could to continue on with my life. Most times it was easier said than done.

Meanwhile, my claim for short-term disability was approved. On September 17th, 1994 Tracey and I were married. The wedding took place at Ebenezer Second Baptist church in Lincoln Heights. The majority of those in attendance were family, friends and extended family. Some of the members of BPB got together and went in on a white stretch limousine for Tracey and me. Right before the wedding, some of the guys and I decided to take the limo on a short cruise. During the ride we toasted our friendship. It was at that moment that I realized just how many loved ones I had in my corner and just how many people had my back. Even though I was torn apart inside and I felt like they couldn't begin to understand how I felt, I knew that they had my back. They would certainly be there when I needed them.

Tracey and I could never really express our thanks enough to her mom Betty and my sister Roberta for all they had done to help us with the wedding. I had been off work for some time before my disability kicked in, so we weren't exactly in the best financial shape. Frankly, we really couldn't afford the type of wedding that we both wanted. Thanks to her mom and my sister, our wedding was better than we had imagined. It was unbelievable, just perfect! My sister did an amazing job on the flowers and coordinated the entire event free of charge. The reception was really nice and we truly felt the love that night. We had so many gifts and the cash we received was really a blessing.

When it was all over, the limo dropped Tracey and me off at home. We had a long flight ahead of us the next day. Despite everything that was going on with my job and our finances, Tracey and I managed to save just enough money to take a honeymoon to Cancun Mexico. It wasn't anything extravagant, but it was really nice (My baby girl can work a budget!). With everything that was going on, she was my solid rock. Not once did she complain. Not once did she make me feel less of a man. Not once did she pity me. Throughout this whole ordeal, she continued to love and support me. She needed this trip just as much as I did. Even though she didn't say it, she was stressed also. I could see it on her face and hear it in her voice. We had a great time! It was nice to leave everything behind, even if it was only for a short time.

As usual, all good things must come to an end. It was back to the hard reality that was my life. A few months had passed and Tracey was pregnant. Neither of us could have been any happier. I had a son, but Tracey didn't have any children and wanted so badly to become a mother. We were both looking forward to having another child around the house. Sometimes I would feel as if there was a heavy cloud following me around and I didn't understand what I had done that was so bad that my life was one continuous living nightmare. A month later, we lost the baby. We couldn't understand why. She was in excellent health and the doctor could find no reason for the miscarriage. We were both grieving. My wife needed me and I was trying to be there for her as much as I could, but I didn't know which person I needed to be. Lately I had started to feel as if there were two other people living inside of me. I felt like I was losing my mind. I was trying so hard to deal with the "Fath" situation, now a miscarriage. With BPB I was strong, confident and serious. With my family and friends I was "Mr. didn't have a care in the world". However, when I was alone I was a crying, shaking mess. I couldn't deal with her loss, I didn't know how. What was I supposed to do? Tell her that everything would be all right?

I thought I could just let the pain go. I didn't realize I was just pushing it back and that it would continue to resurface over and over until I dealt with it or at least found a way to deal with it. I know that I wasn't there for her the way she needed me to be. I wanted to be there for her but I couldn't. I didn't even know who I was anymore. I was slowly being ripped apart and I couldn't stop it. Life was starting to have no meaning for me. Life no longer mattered. I had put so much into this company and to be treated like a stray dog by people that I considered decent. It was tearing me apart. I tried so hard to just let it go, to move forward. I couldn't just leave the feelings I was having behind. I did everything I could. I saw my Dr. as often as I could. I prayed daily for God to stop the pain. I even tried burying myself in the organization. Nothing was working. I felt like I was being eaten from the inside out.

I was a survivor. Here I was someone who had survived and made it out of one of the biggest, toughest projects in this city. I had so much pride, so much strength. Where was that strength now that I really needed it? I was broken. I felt so bad one night that I just wanted the hurt to stop. I was feeling more depressed than ever and had been out driving by myself for some time. My eyes were bloodshot from all the crying I had been doing and my head was pounding. I thought back on my life and couldn't figure things out. I was always the kind of person who thought of others first. I was a good person. No, I wasn't perfect and I had made many mistakes along the way. But I couldn't understand why God was allowing the pain to continue. What had I done to upset him so badly? Why was God punishing me? I couldn't do it anymore. I couldn't continue to live, not like this. There was too much pain.

That night when I got home, I went up to my bedroom and pulled out my gun. As I raised the gun to my head, I saw my life clearly. I saw all the wonderful things that I had. I couldn't give up that easily. Even though the pain was often unbearable and it preoccupied my mind almost every waking moment of my life, I couldn't give up that easily. At that moment, Tracey walked into the room. I sat there crying with the gun in my hands. We both stared at the gun and cried. I let it all out; I told her how I was feeling. She gave me a hug and said that things would get better.

Unfortunately, things got worse. Tracey was pregnant again and the doctor had put her on complete bed rest. The one saving grace was that her job covered it completely. Tracey was about five months pregnant when she had another miscarriage. This time it was worse than the first and it hit me pretty hard also. It only made me feel worse when the doctor told us that it was stress related. I blamed myself for Tracey's miscarriages. Tracey was under stress because of my problems. Tracey and I didn't talk to anyone about our problems. We kept them in our home and between the two of us. Although it wasn't our way to put our problems out there for everyone to see, our families knew that things weren't right. They weren't sure exactly what was going on, but they knew we were going through some real trials.

I never told Dr. Thomas or anyone about the gun incident. First, I was ashamed of it. I couldn't believe that I had allowed myself to become so weak. Secondly, sometimes I felt as if I was losing my mind. I was afraid that Dr. Thomas would see me as a threat to others or myself and have me committed somewhere. The one thing that I was sure of is that I had some serious issues that I had to deal with. First and foremost was my work situation.

Why was my life in constant turmoil? My wife and I were both stressed beyond belief. We both felt strongly that stress was the cause for both of her miscarriages. I was at the point where I didn't trust any person whose skin was white or anything closely resembling white. I couldn't deal with them. I felt as if they all had contributed to my wife's hardships and mine. Surely, they were all to blame. I shared this with Dr. Thomas and he assured me that, in time, this feeling would go away.

I had to let go. I had to stop believing that I was being punished for something. I had to start looking at God as my healer and not my punisher. Tracey and I would pray together at home, at church, and in the car, wherever we could. We prayed that God would come into our lives and help us. We asked him to bless us with a baby girl. I also asked God to give me the strength to go on with my life and give me the strength I was going to need to stand up for myself and my God given rights. I was going to stand up for what I believed and I was going to fight. I asked God to give me my day in court and that His will be done. Win or lose, just give me a chance to fight back and be heard. Whatever the outcome, I would be satisfied because it would be God's will. I just wanted the chance to make them see what they had done to me. I wanted them to stand and face me and tell me why. I wanted Fath to hear my words and I wanted them to look me in my face for once.

I had no choice but to take Fath Management to the United States District Court, charging them with discrimination. I wasn't just doing it for my family and myself, but for all the other people of color who would be treated the same way I had been treated. I knew that with God, I couldn't lose.

"Once again, I had been stabbed in the back and although my spirits were down, they weren't broken."

Chapter 8

Deception

Black Positive Brothers was really on the move. Men were coming from all over wanting to be a part of the organization. Of course, we were more than happy to have their support.

Our organization accepted members from a variety of backgrounds and there was one member in particular that was heavily involved in the political arena. His name was Melvin. Melvin was so into politics that we appointed him to the position of political advisor. He seemed to have the community's best interest at heart. I personally initiated this move. Melvin's job was to gather information on various local candidates running for office along with any relevant political issues. He would then present the information at our meetings once every two months. This was a way to provide our members with valuable information on the candidates and to ensure that everyone was well informed.

What Melvin didn't know was that the BPB board was comprised of family, close long time friends, and very loyal members. From the start, at least a few members came to me confidentially and told me that they didn't trust this brother. They couldn't quite put their finger on what bothered them so much about Melvin, but they knew something wasn't right with him. I would always blow this kind of talk off. Melvin was doing his job. He was educating our members on the political scene in our city and our region.

Occasionally members would come to me and express their concerns about Melvin acting as if he were positioning himself to take over control of BPB. Melvin taking control of the group definitely wasn't something that these members were going to take lightly. They didn't trust this guy and they weren't willing to let him lead the organization. I reassured the brothers that this was not an option and that the foundation for BPB had been set. Nothing was going to change. I had built BPB on the love that I had for my community and its people. It had been founded on trust and friendship. I knew that God had my back, so I wasn't worried about what Melvin was or wasn't going to do.

As part of being a member of Black Positive Brothers, each member had to do his part to support the organization financially. This meant that each member was expected to pay his monthly dues. The funds we collected helped the organization to support the community projects we had going on at the time and helped us to plan future projects. We had a lot on our plates and no financial backing. Black Positive Brothers was one aspect of my life that I was really proud of; BPB meant so much to me. It wasn't long before Satan would find a way to come in and try to destroy the one thing that was holding me together.

In any organization, you will always find those individuals who want to be associated with something that is good and is recognized and appreciated by the community, but they aren't willing to support the organization financially. Melvin was one of those individuals. He may have paid his dues once or twice, but nothing more.

In November of 1995, BPB was scheduled to deliver Thanksgiving baskets to needy local families in conjunction with one of the local radio stations here in Cincinnati. On my way out to meet the representatives from the radio station, I stopped to check the mail. Inside my mailbox, I found an envelope addressed to me from Melvin. I took a brief moment to read the letter before heading to the radio station. Wow! Talk about timing! In the letter, Melvin made the claim that I was using the money the organization collected from monthly membership dues and fundraisers for my own personal needs. I really didn't need this right now. I was on my way to meet the members at the radio station and I needed to be in the right frame of mind.

I was not in the best of moods when I pulled up to the radio station. As luck would have it, who is it I see as I am getting out of my car? I was steaming! Melvin spotted me and he tried to hurry into the radio station. At that very moment, I saw the sneaky and conniving person that my members had been warning me about. I caught Melvin before he got into the station and I went off on him right there in the parking lot! While I was ripping Melvin a new behind, I didn't notice that our newly appointed president Moe had pulled up and was fast approaching us. Moe had gotten the letter, as had every other member in Black Positive Brothers. Moe and I had grown up together and had become best friends over the years. He knew that he needed to get there before me. Moe jumped in between Melvin and me trying to diffuse the situation. I couldn't believe this! I had been in Melvin's corner the entire time! When the other members wanted him gone, I stood by him. Melvin just stood there in his BPB jacket and beret, speechless and looking stupid. Once again, I had been stabbed in the back and although my spirits were down, they weren't broken. Moe turned to me and told me to let it go. We went on inside to do what we had promised we would do. Just as quickly as the letter had arrived, Melvin disappeared. He was gone.

We went to each family's house and dropped off the baskets. It was difficult seeing the bad living conditions that the families had to endure. This is what it's really all about though: helping someone who needs and wants your help. I wasn't angry with Melvin anymore. My heart knew that this had happened for the good. If his heart had been in it for the community, Melvin would never have attacked BPB the way he did. If he had concerns, he could have expressed them at the next meeting. No concern was off limits as far as our organization was concerned. Melvin knew exactly what he was doing. By destroying the foundation, he felt he could rebuild the group the way he wanted. His biggest mistake was assuming that the members had no faith or trust in me.

That following Sunday I called a special meeting to address the issues that Melvin had brought up in his letter to all the members. The members of BPB were beyond furious with him. The meeting was to be held at the Woodlawn Municipal Building where we always held our meetings. I took my time getting there once church was out. I wanted to give the members time to get there. By the time I arrived at the meeting, all the members were already there, including Melvin. As soon as I walked through the door, before we could even start the meeting, my members told me to just leave it alone. They said we didn't need the meeting and that I didn't have to explain or prove anything to anyone.

I insisted on proceeding with the meeting. I would not have been at ease until I had dealt with this issue head on.

Normally, when we have our meetings, the five board members sit at one long table up front facing the general members. On this day I stood up front alone, facing all the members. I felt like I was in court having to defend myself. I started off by stating a very important fact to the members. I told them that we had four other board members, one of which was the treasurer. No one, and I mean no one, is about to let me spend money that belongs to the organization. There were too many checks and balances.

Next, I addressed Melvin. I asked him, "are you on our Finance Committee?" His reply was "no." I asked him, "have you ever seen our financial statements?" Once again, his reply was "no." I asked him, "then what gives you the right to dispense such a letter?" Of course he couldn't give me an answer. Right after that, one of the members stood up and verbally attacked Melvin. One by one, the rest of the members started in on him. They couldn't believe we were wasting our time on this. We never had much money coming in to begin with. Remember, not all the members were paying their dues and at that time, we didn't have any financial support from the community. So where was all this money that I was allegedly taking coming from? All the members knew that we were putting the money out into the communities as quickly as we were receiving it.

The entire time this was going on, Melvin had three members who were in his corner all the way, Cal, Jeff and Tim. I'll give it to Melvin; he didn't go into this blindly. He did his research. He tried to get as many members on his side as he could. It's pretty pathetic that out of the forty or so men who were members at that time, Melvin could only manipulate three of them into sharing his position.

Tim was Melvin's best friend. In fact, they had joined the group together. Jeff had just gotten out of prison. I brought him into BPB trying to help him out in life and give him some sense of direction. As far as Jeff was concerned, I could have taken the attitude that you get what you ask for. However, I wouldn't say that because that was one of our goals: To help those who had fallen. I didn't know that much about Cal. I did know that he was very well educated and extremely smart. We all know someone like Cal: very intelligent, but no commonsense at all. That was Cal. After that meeting on Sunday, Melvin and the other three never did return to the organization. I guess they were too embarrassed. Either way, the problem had been dealt with. Black Positive Brothers business went on as usual.

"A man's weakness can become the beginning of a man's strength."

Chapter 9

Closure

While I was off on sick leave, I had gone to the U.S. Equal Employment Opportunity Commission, to file a discrimination complaint against Fath Management. I was determined to stand up for my rights. This company had done me wrong because of the color of my skin and I was not going to stand for it.

Around October of 1995, Dr. John Thomas and I felt that it was time for me to return to work. I was starting to feel like my old self again. Some would have said that I should have just moved on and found another job. Because of the type of person I am, I couldn't do that. I needed some kind of closure to this. I also knew that I would have just taken my problem to the next job. I had finally overcome my problem of disliking all white people. I had always known that all white people were not bad, just as all blacks aren't bad. But I had also realized that your own personal problems could blind you to that fact.

I reported back to work first thing on October 2nd 1995. No one said anything to me or told me what to do. I was just informed by letter that I was back in the Maintenance Department under the supervision of Dan Little. Dan Little was the new supervisor that I had trained to do my job. So you can imagine what that did to me inside. I just had to stay strong.

Since no one had given me any instructions on what to do, I got my own work orders out of the outgoing ticket box and went on my way. By the third day, Jeff, one of the managers, called me into the office and I was told that I wasn't doing enough work. Jeff was writing me up for this. I said to Jeff that "no one had given me any work assignments or told me what to do. So how could you write me up?" "No one ever said "glad you're back" or "How are you doing" or anything. But I was supposed to know how much work you wanted me to do?" I did not sign the papers. I became very upset. Once again, my doctor put me on sick leave. By March, another letter came from my company stating that if I didn't return to work, I would be fired. Meanwhile, right when my doctor put me back on sick leave for the second time, I filed another discrimination charge with the EEOC.

Although my doctor wouldn't discharge me, I went back to work. I knew that I needed my job to help support my family. Needless to say, I was fired for not having a release from my doctor. You would have thought that I would have become angry or upset from being fired, but I wasn't. That dark cloud over my head was gone. It was as if God had answered my prayers in taking away the hurt and pain. I had closure. I could now move forward with the rest of my life.

"We must never give up!"

Chapter 10

Black Men on the Move

In 1995, Black Positive Brothers was planning a trip to the "Million Man March". The march was being held in the nation's capital, Washington D.C. Thousands of black men from all across the country were expected to attend. The Nation of Islam leader, Minister Louis Farrakhan was the keynote speaker and event organizer. The streets of Washington were jammed packed; brothers were standing shoulder to shoulder. There were black men from all walks of life there. The day was extremely powerful. Brothers were kind and polite to one another. I could not believe my eyes. It was as if God had touched every Black man that was there.

There were more than 24 different speakers delivering a common message: that it was time for black men to stop tearing down and start helping to rebuild. Rebuild our communities, families and the country we live in. Our job was to go back to our communities and take care of our families, start organizations to help rebuild our communities, do our part to stop black-on-black violence and help clean up the drugs. I thought, "Yes!" I was so glad that I was there to hear and see it. It was powerful and sometimes overwhelming, but it was truly a blessing. Black Positive Brothers were already ahead of the game. We were already active in our community, helping to rebuild and restore. I left the march with the assurance that if we as black men did our part; our communities would overcome and begin to flourish.

The weekend was over and I was back home. All the problems that I had left behind during the march were still there, but the spirit of the march was still with me. I knew that God had not forgotten me. I was not a Muslim and I had never personally met Honorable Minister Louis Farrakhan, but I had nothing but a great deal of respect for this Black man. To do something so positive and so powerful as bringing together black men from all walks of life and to send them back home with a mission. It was truly a great thing!

Black Positive Brothers was really on the move. Those of us who had attended the Million Man March really put forth an effort to come back to our communities and apply some of the things that Minister Farrakhan had spoken about in his address. For example, the City of Lincoln Heights was in need of a concession stand for their youth sports programs. At the time, they didn't have the money in the city budget to build a new one. Black Positive Brothers sponsored the concession stand. We purchased all the materials and members donated a lot of their time to build the stand. In addition, Black Positive Brothers visited different urban schools and talked to students about the problems that were destroying our communities. We spoke with the kids about how important it was for them to stay focused and we shared some of our stories and pitfalls. We encouraged them to strive for success in whatever they decided to do.

In January of 1996, Black Positive Brothers took a trip to Atlanta in honor of Dr. Martin Luther King Jr.'s birthday. Personally, this trip to Atlanta had a lot more meaning than the first two trips I had taken. With all that my wife and I had been through over the past year or so, I had a better understanding of Dr. King's pain and frustration. I could imagine the emotional and physical fatigue he must have felt. The struggles taking place in our community were much more meaningful to me.

One of my long time friends was a member of Black Positive Brothers and had been living in Atlanta for some time now. While in Atlanta, we proudly walked around the city wearing our berets. Everyone we encountered wanted to know more about the organization. We investigated the possibility of starting a BPB Chapter in Atlanta, but things didn't quite work out. A Black Positive Brothers chapter in Atlanta would have been really successful. Now that I actually think about it, maybe it would have been more successful in Atlanta than in Cincinnati. For some reason, the blacks in Atlanta seemed to be a little more supportive than those in Cincinnati.

Shortly after returning home, we began preparations for our First Annual Awards Banquet. The banquet was being held to recognize those students who had overcome the odds and dealt with the many obstacles in their lives to become successful productive students. We had held an essay contest in order to identify potential student honorees. We sent applications to guidance counselors at several different schools around the city. The guidance counselors then passed the applications on to students who fit our criteria.

The banquet was a great success! The support and sponsorship that we received from the business community was excellent. We had a lot of special guests and the media covered the event. Black Positive Brothers helped me to uncover all those hidden talents you hear people talk so much about. I discovered that I really had a talent for Marketing and Planning.

After the awards banquet, Moe and I were being asked to attend all sorts of political events around the city. I chose to attend a few events, but typically I would politely decline the invitation. Black Positive Brothers was not a political organization; it was a grass roots community organization. I didn't want Black Positive Brothers to get caught up in the political arena. There was too much that needed to be done in the community for me to spend my time sitting in meetings. I always made sure that my vote was cast and I tried to make sure that the members were well informed, but that was the extent of it. BPB was not a political organization.

Our next event was coming up fast. We had planned an Anti-Drug and Violence Rally at one of our local High Schools. The High School was an inner-city school in the Cincinnati Public School district. An overwhelming majority of the students there were black. The school wasn't without its problems. Right around the time we had decided to do the rally, a student was shot right across the street from the school. It was a sad case of being in the wrong place at the wrong time. The bullet missed its intended target and struck the student, who was one of the many students watching the entire incident unfold.

The BPB rally was held on the football field. We had several different speakers speak on the problems that were destroying our communities. Cincinnati Police Captain, Ron Twitty handed out information on drugs, violence and some of the many other problems going on within our communities.

I had the pleasure of meeting Captain Twitty sometime ago and he, along with some of his other officers, had been very supportive of Black Positive Brothers. Whenever we needed a speaker to talk to our youth or to hand out information, they were always helpful. With the help of different community organizations, the rally was excellent! We had free food and t-shirts. Several youth groups performed singing, dancing, and rapping. The rally was very successful, but this wasn't the only rally we would hold. There were many other rallies held around the city. If Black Positive Brothers could reach just a handful of these kids, then all the hard work and dedication was more than worth it.

Thanks to God and the love and support of family and friends, my hard work and dedication to Black Positive Brothers was not going unnoticed. I had won several awards. In July 1995, I was awarded the WCIN Radio/ Bank One "Citizen of the Week"; in February of 1996, the 3Square Music Foundation awarded a "Certificate of Achievement" to Black Positive Brothers for "Supporters of the Year". In May 1996 I received the Unsung Hero award from the radio station WIZF. It was a very busy time for me. I was doing a lot of television talk shows, radio shows, and newspaper and magazine articles. Essence magazine also did a small article on the BPB organization and me. Black Positive Brothers was definitely on the move.

"I was really learning to depend on God more."

Chapter 11

Prayers Answered

I was really learning to depend on God more. Tracey and I had hung a "Serenity Prayer" plaque in our bathroom and we would refer to it daily. At the time, we were constantly praying for God to bless us with a healthy baby girl. We had gone through so much, including the miscarriages. I could look into Tracey's eyes and see that she was losing faith.

Now Tracey was pregnant for the third time. Because of the prior miscarriages, Tracey's doctor put her on part-time duty at work for the duration of her pregnancy. Tracey was several months into her pregnancy and was doing just fine. It looked like we were really going to make it this time. We were finally going to have the baby we both wanted so much. If we were blessed with a girl, we had decided on the name Serenity (after the prayer). We had no name picked out for a boy; we wanted a little girl. On October 20th 1996, God answered our prayers and blessed us with a healthy baby girl. Her name: Serenity Ebonay Wiley. Finally, we had peace and grace!

In March of 1996, my doctor gave me the okay to return to work. I didn't have a job to go back to, but that didn't last long. A couple of months after being released by my doctor, I landed a job with Metro Prop. Realty. One of my old friends from Fath was working there. He had come over to visit me and he had mentioned that they were looking for a maintenance technician.

Prior to hearing about this job opening, I was getting somewhat discouraged. Everyone was turning me down. I knew I was qualified, and I knew that companies were looking to hire. What was going on? One of the owners of Metro Prop. Realty was Mr. K. The property manager was a man by the name of Jack. My friend had told them about my qualifications and my experience. Jack interviewed me and things went well. So well in fact, that he said that Mr. K. also wanted to interview me. At the end of the interview, he informed me that the job was mine (Hey, the starting pay was good).

Shortly after starting my new job, I met the new leasing agent Ann. She seemed like a really nice person. She was very religious. She attended church every chance she got. One day, a well-known evangelist from Florida was in town and Ann invited me to her church. When Ann and I arrived at the church, they were having prayer request up front. I felt compelled to go up for prayer. The evangelist picked me out of the audience with a message, a prophecy for me. He said that there would be thousands and thousands of kids who would be coming to me. I had always believed in God, but I was unsure about prophesying. The next day at work, Ann came in and was still very excited about what the evangelist had said to me the night before. Truthfully, I hadn't given it a second thought. I told Ann that I was giving serious thought to starting Black Positive Sisters. I told her that I thought she would be perfect for the position of president. She was more than flattered and accepted.

During this time in my life, I was still attending two churches: the church where I had grown up, (Ebenezer Second Baptist Church) and the church I had found as an adult, (Revelation Church of God). One Sunday, my family and I decided to go to Revelation Church of God. Pastor Matt was leading prayer when he just stopped in the middle of his prayer and asked me to come up to the front. He had a message for me. He said that God was going to bless me with a very large sum of money and that it wasn't coming from where I thought it was. The first thing that came to my mind was my Fath case; however, he had just said that it wasn't coming from where I thought it was coming from.

I was starting to become well-known around the Cincinnati area. I received several invitations to different charity fundraisers and community programs. Someone that I had gotten to know through Black Positive Brothers invited me to be one of the ten judges for a black history costume contest. I almost decided not to go, but for some reason, I just felt like I had to be there. At the time, Tracey and I were still living on Fath Property and we were no longer getting the discounted rent we once received. We were paying the full rental amount and money was tight. At the program that night, I met a gentleman by the name of Kelly. He asked me if I owned a home. I told him that I didn't and that I wasn't interested in one right now, but I gave him one of my business cards anyway. At the time, I had so many things going on. Our budget was limited. A new home just wasn't a part of our immediate plans. Kelly was really persistent though. He called Tracey and me consistently for about a month. Finally, we agreed to go in and speak with him. As it turns out, this was a good decision. Within two months of Kelly and my initial visit, Tracey and I were in the process of having a four-bedroom home built from the ground up.

The best part is that we only had to put down $7,000.00 and our interest rate was a moderate 6.5% fixed. Not too bad for what the house was worth.

Tracey and I decided to get rid of our current vehicle. We purchased a 1993 Cadillac Danderville, fully loaded. God was really blessing our lives. It was nice to finally have some joy. Isn't God good!

At that time, Tracey and I had also made another big decision. We decided that it was time that my son Anthony came to live with us. Anthony, whom we affectionately called "Ant", had started giving his mother some problems. Anthony had been with Kathy for the last 10 years so the time was right. He needed me on a full time basis now. When Kathy came to me and told me that she just couldn't handle him anymore and that he needed to be with me, I was more than happy to oblige. Anthony had picked up quite a few bad habits and I was hoping that we could change some of that.

God had really and truly blessed Tracey and me. We had prayed for so long for all the wonderful things that we were now enjoying in our life. We had a new baby girl, my son was living with us on a full-time basis, I had a new job, and our new home. The one important lesson it taught me is that God will give you the things your heart truly desires, but only in his time, not yours. God will give you what you desire, when and only when he sees that you are ready to receive them. God had also given me back my life that Fath had stripped from me. God had restored my self-esteem, my pride and my confidence. He restored these things in a way that made me feel as though I was on top of the world.

"To God Be The Glory"

Chapter 12

God Continues to Bless Us

Living on Fath Management's Property had become very uncomfortable, almost unbearable. Tracey and I couldn't wait for the builders to finish our home. Just when we thought we couldn't take any more, Tracey's mom opened her doors to us. She asked us if we wanted to move into her home until our house had been completed. We jumped at the opportunity: we really needed to get out of our current living situation. Not only did my wife's mother offer us a place to live but she also told us that it wasn't necessary to pay her anything. This way we could keep our money and save it to purchase new furniture. After thanking her for her generosity, we couldn't move in fast enough!

By this time I was attending Revelation Church of God on a regular basis. I was very much involved in church again. One particular Sunday, Pastor Matt prophesied on me again and said that he saw me dealing with thousands of children. He also said that he saw me on the front cover of Time Magazine. I was truly amazed! "How could this be true?" What I was involved in at the time was small-time in comparison to what Pastor Matt was seeing. It wasn't so much that I doubted Pastor Matt's gift of prophecies; I just didn't understand it. However, I really put some deep thought into what Pastor Matt was telling me. This wasn't

the first time that a man of God spoke to me about a prophecy. Several months earlier, we had a guest speaker at church.
He was an evangelist from Chicago who said that he knew
I was involved with a group that was doing some very important work. He went on to say there would come a day
when I would break all ties with the group and its people;
that I would move on. He said that there would be a new
group of people that I would be working with. I thought to
myself, "this man doesn't even know me. Could someone
have told him about my work with BPB?"

Tracey and I were only two days away from closing
on our brand new home. We were so excited. I couldn't believe it! In just a couple of days we would be in our own
home. That evening Tracey and I were relaxing at home
when the phone rang. Tracey answered the phone, and I
could tell by the look on her face that they weren't calling
us to congratulate us on the purchase of our new home. The
mortgage lender from Indianapolis had called to tell us that
they had made a mistake. We were told that they should
have added another three thousand more dollars onto our
house loan for our down payment. We would have to come
up with this amount before we could close on our home.
Tracey was so upset. She told them that we didn't have another three thousand dollars to give. She told them that we
had already given up our apartment, that all of our things
were in storage and we were living with her mother. The
Mortgage Company could care less what our current situation was.

Tracey handed me the phone. She just couldn't
deal with it anymore. By this time, she was completely in
tears. Now it was my turn to have a conversation with the
Mortgage Company. Before they could repeat to me what

they had told Tracey, I let them know that they were the ones who had made the mistake and that they needed to live up to it and honor our agreement. I asked them how could they call us two days before closing and actually expect us to pull another three thousand dollars out of thin air. I told them we didn't have it and couldn't get it. Their response was that if we didn't have it, we couldn't move in. Needless to say, that was the end of the phone conversation.

Tracey and I didn't even have half of what they were asking for. We had just purchased brand new furniture: living room suit, dining room suit and a new bedroom suit. We had essentially used all the extra money we had saved. Besides, this was the mortgage company's fault, not ours. Tracey and I knew that this home and our baby girl were true blessings from God and no one could take either of them from us. We were so upset and there was nothing we could do. We couldn't give them what we didn't have. We just prayed over it and released it by faith. God would handle it. On the morning we were due to close, the Mortgage Company called. They had decided to take a loss on the three thousand dollars. We were going to be able to close on our home that night after all. Isn't God grand? Just when it seems hopeless, he comes through.

The next day Tracey and I started moving into our new home, with the help of some of the BPB members and a few other friends. One of the oldest members of BPB, Dwayne, bought us a garage door opener as a house warming present. Dwayne's generosity didn't stop there. He told me to go and pick out any pool table that I wanted for my basement and it was mine. Tracey and I both thanked him. We were so grateful that he did this for us.

BPB started a co-ed softball team. We chose the name "Black Positive Ballers". In September, we had our 3rd Annual Family and Friends cookout. The event included free food, free games, and free toys for the kids. On this day, our softball team was set to play one of the best co-ed teams in the city, WIZF the Wiz. Well, they were the best. They hadn't played us yet: of course, we won the game! 1997 was a good year for Black Positive Brothers and Sisters. I continued to receive recognition for my contributions to Black Positive Brothers and Sisters. I received the "Applause Image Makers" award for emerging leader. I received personal congratulatory letters from both United States Senator Mike DeWine and Congressman Steve Chabot.

We also held our 2nd Annual Awards Banquet that year. We honored eight deserving students from different areas in Cincinnati. These kids had really gotten their act together! Each one had challenges academically and personally at one time or another, but each managed to pull things together and become a successful student. We wanted to do something really special for them so we hired a stretch limousine to pick them up and chauffeur them to the awards banquet. We were all proud of them and the work they had put in. 1997 was a year that I will never forget.

"To be racist or prejudiced is to hate yourself."

Chapter 13

Waiting for Right to Sue Letter

Everything was going pretty well in my life, all things considered. I had a loyal and loving family and I had full custody of my son (My ex-wife and I still weren't getting along, but you can't always have everything). It was a struggle trying to get Anthony focused on school; but that was nothing new. I had always had trouble out of him when it came to academics. It was really frustrating. Anthony is the type of kid that has great potential. He's very intelligent, but he always spent too much time playing around. Sometimes, I would visit his class and sit in on some of the lessons. Of course he was on his best behavior when I was there. Now when I wasn't there, that was a completely different story! Tracey would sometimes ask me if I wanted more kids, but my answer was always the same. I knew that she wanted more children, but I had my son and daughter and didn't see the need for more. Besides, I never wanted to have a lot of children. Children are no joke; it takes a lot to raise them.

It had been a while since I filed my complaint against Fath Management with the Equal Employment Opportunity Commission. Occasionally I would call just to get an update on how the investigation was going. I learned that the process is not always simple. The job of the EEOC is two-fold. First, they must determine if discrimination did actually occur. Secondly, they have to determine if there is enough information for you to move forward. If they're able to prove these two things in your favor, they then send you a "Right to Sue" letter enabling you to proceed with your lawsuit. The company or individual in question would have two choices: they could go to methods of conciliation with you or they could just opt to take their chances in Federal court.

It was January 1998 when I received two letters from EEOC. I ran into the house with the letters so Tracey and I could read them together. This was what I had been waiting for. It had taken several years just to get to this point and there was still a long road ahead. I guess Tracey got tired of me sitting there holding the letters, because she finally asked, "Well, are you going to open them?" I was so nervous. I didn't know what I was going to do if I opened the letters and they weren't in my favor. I read the first letter. It said that they found in my favor regarding the second part of my complaint. They had determined that there was retaliation on the part of Fath Management for my having filed a previous complaint. I opened the second letter. God is good! In the second letter, they said that they had found in my favor regarding the first half of my complaint. They said that they could find no reason other than my race for me to have been demoted and replaced by my Caucasian co-worker. I couldn't believe it! The wait was over! I could now move forward with my case.

Shortly after receiving my letters, EEOC contacted me and informed me that Fath Management was not interested in conciliation. They knew that I would have to obtain an attorney to handle my case. I wanted an African-American attorney. Even though I had gotten over feeling as if I couldn't trust Caucasians, I needed an African-American attorney. I needed someone who knew from the soul where I was coming from and could relate to what I had gone through. I wanted someone who didn't have any doubts as to what had happened to me. I wanted someone who wouldn't see me as a disgruntled employee who now wanted to "play the race card" to cover up his sloppy work habits.

The first attorney I checked out wanted entirely too much money up front. I wanted one that would work on a contingency base only. The second guy I checked out really didn't seem too sure of himself. My believing the way that I do, I prayed on it. I started going through the yellow pages looking for an attorney. I came across "Lyons & Fries Co., LPA. That is where I met Attorney James D. Ludwig (He was a Caucasian). Mr. Ludwig and I got together and after speaking with him, I knew that he was the man for me. He took my case. I still had to pay a fee, but it was significantly lower than the fee the other two lawyers wanted me to pay. Also, I didn't have to come up with the entire balance before he could start on my case. He worked with me and I was able to pay him monthly. It was on now! I was finally going to have my day in court. This company almost destroyed my life. They got me to a point where I was ready to take my life. They were going to hear from me and it was going to be in front of a Federal judge.

James D. Ludwig was a polite and knowledgeable man. I actually enjoyed working on the case with him. I can remember one meeting in particular. We were in his office discussing the case, and Mr. Ludwig stepped out to get me something to drink. I don't know why, but I thought back to when I was blaming all whites for my problems during the time I was seeing Dr. Thomas. It scared me. It really scared me. I couldn't believe that I had let Fath turn me into the type of person that they did back then. I hated an entire race of people because of something that one company had done to me. I thank God that he led me to Dr. Thomas. What was so ironic about the entire situation was that my own people had openly discriminated against me. There were blacks who treated me badly simply because I was darker skinned, but I never hated blacks as a whole. It feels good to be well again.

My trial was set for October 2000. I would finally get Fath Management where I had been working to get them for the past several years: in front of a jury at the United States District Court, Southern District of Ohio Western Division.

"I looked each and every one of the officers that were standing around right in their face and I told them that they didn't hurt me and they couldn't take anything away from me. I told them that these tears were for every black man they had unjustly treated this way."

Chapter 14

Cincinnati Police Brutality

My family and I had just gotten back from vacation. Although we had a great time and I really enjoyed the time I had spent with my family, it was a long trip and I needed a little time to myself. I decided to go to a little neighborhood club not far from my home. I wanted to play a couple games of pool with some friends of mine. I played pool for a couple of hours before deciding to go home. While on my way out, a lady approached me about becoming a member of Black Positive Sisters. We both were on our way out, so I told her to follow me to my car and I would get a business card for her and she could call the office and get more information. I was parked in the lot at the back of the club and she was parked on the street in front of the club. Since I was going that way, I told her to get in and I would give her a ride to her car, which was only a short distance from where we were.

Just as we both got into the car, two gentlemen started knocking on my car window. I knew who they were and what they wanted as soon as they walked up to my car. I let my window down and one of them explained that they had gotten a call regarding someone in a white Cadillac smoking crack in the back parking lot. That's right; the two gentlemen who were knocking on my window were plain-clothes policemen (Now before I go any further, I should mention that my Cadillac was very nice. It was a four-door luxury model with tinted windows, white wall tires with chrome wheels and chrome trim around the bottom of the car from the front to the back. There was nothing about my car that said, "man on crack"). In actuality, there was no call about a man smoking crack. These two individuals saw what they thought was a black man who sold drugs and they needed an excuse, any excuse, to approach me.

I told the two officers that they couldn't have gotten a call about me smoking crack in my car because first and most important, I didn't do drugs. Secondly, no one and I do mean no one, smokes in my car. Besides, if I had been smoking with the windows up, the smoke and smell would have hit them directly in their faces when I let the windows down. Neither of the officers was trying to hear what I was saying. They were going in one direction and they weren't about to be side tracked… even if it was apparent that their explanation for questioning me was way off base.

One of the officers ordered me to get out of the car. The young lady that I had offered a ride to was still in the car with me while all this was going down. She also got out of the car. The officers then asked me if they could search my car. What was my reply? "No way!" They had no valid reason to search my car. At this point, one of the officers started to pat me down and check to make sure that I didn't have any weapons. The entire time they are patting me down and checking for weapons, they are continuously asking me if they can search my car. My answer was the same each and every time. Finally, one of the officers said that if I didn't give them permission to search the car, they were going to call in the drug dogs and search it anyway.

I asked the officer if it were that simple, then why were they even asking my permission to search.

When my family and I went on vacation, I took my .25 caliber handgun along with us. The gun was locked in the trunk and the clip was locked in the glove compartment. I told the officer about the firearm being in the trunk and the clip being in the glove compartment. Well, that was all they needed to hear. He ordered me to turn around and put both hands behind my back. He slammed the cuffs on me. The cuffs were extremely tight and pretty painful. My request to have them loosened was totally ignored. The officers searched my car from front to back. The only thing they found was the firearm and clip and they were exactly where I told them they were.

The officers then turned their attention to the young lady that was being detained with me as well. I heard one of the officers ask her where she had gotten all the cash she had on her. She told them that she owns a hair boutique and had earned the money. She then sarcastically asked the officer if that was all right with him. I couldn't see her from where I was, but I knew they were searching her also. My wrists were killing me. The cuffs were really tight. I complained again that the cuffs were too tight, but again, I was ignored. By this time, police vehicles were everywhere! The two officers put me into the back of one of the cruisers and asked the female officer to run my license through and see if anything comes back. He asked me if my firearm was registered and I told him it was. I wasn't worried. My gun was clean. It was registered and it was legal for me to carry. I told the officers again that my cuffs were too tight. This time, he responded. He took the cuffs off and replaced them with another pair, just as tight as the first pair. I didn't get it. What was the point of replacing one pair with another if you were going to put the replacement pair on just as tight as the original?

It had been about an hour and a half and they must have run my license through the system about five times. I overheard the officer whisper to the female officer "no felonies?" I heard her tell him that I didn't have any felonies. Finally! They had no choice but to let me out of the cruiser and take the cuffs off. My wrists were killing me. I don't know which pain was worse, the pain in my wrists or the humiliation. There were cops all around, just standing. There was one African-American cop out of the whole bunch. I turned to him and I said, "you see what they did to me?" He didn't say a word; he just turned his back to me.

I asked the two officers who had originally set off this entire drama for their badge numbers. They refused to give them to me. The Sergeant who had arrived on the scene shortly after it began told me that I couldn't have their badge numbers, but I could have his. By this time, the tears were coming down my face. I told him that I didn't want his badge number. I wanted the badge numbers of the two officers that did this to me. The Sergeant told me "no" and if I didn't shut up and leave right now, he would arrest me for disorderly conduct.

I looked each and every one of the officers that were standing around right in their face and I told them that they didn't hurt me and they couldn't take anything away from me. I told them that these tears were for every black man they had unjustly treated this way. The Sergeant was pissed off completely by this time. He was screaming at me like you wouldn't believe, becoming more and more aggravated.

He was just looking for a reason to arrest me. I think my actions are what upset him so much. He had expected me to act unruly and indignant. He expected me to act crazy. When I didn't, he didn't have a reason to take me in. This meant he, and his officers would not be able to save face. Now the shoe was on the other foot. You see it was all right when they had me cuffed and caged in the back of the squad car like a caged animal for all to see. They never thought they would have to let me go. They just knew they had a criminal. Now, they were ticked off because they had nothing. I watched them watch me as I drove away with my .25 still locked in the trunk of the car. I watched them watching me drive away knowing that they had nothing and couldn't do anything. Right afterwards, I went down to District 5 and filed a formal complaint against the Cincinnati Police Department.

The next day my entire arm was swollen and painful. I couldn't lift nor do anything with my right hand. My wife insisted that I go to the emergency room. I wasn't trying to hear it. I would be all right, no big deal. By the next day, I was in so much pain that I had no choice. I was unable to function. All I could think about was the pain. Tracey drove me to the emergency room. My wrist and arm were examined and X-rayed. The doctor said that I had a really bad sprain. He put my arm in a sling and told me to wear it for the next 4 to 6 weeks. I was furious! I went to the Office of the Municipal Investigations (OMI) and filed a complaint about the incident. It was OMI's job to conduct an investigation into what had happened between the officers and me. Here we go again. Why can't I just have a normal life free from drama? My case with Fath Management hadn't even really gotten started and here I was again.

I asked myself if it was something that I was doing to make people treat me so badly. I knew that it was just the nature of some people to think that they were better than others were simply because they were a different color. It was easier for me to deal with an open racist than an undercover racist. At least when you deal with an open racist you know exactly where you stand. They don't pretend or try to convince you that what they are doing they are doing for reasons other than your color. They let you know up front. They'll tell you that they don't like you and they have no purpose for you so it's best that the two of you don't cross paths or even try and pretend to be civil to one another. It's best to just stay out of each other's way. But it's the undercover racist in positions of power and authority that can and do the most damage. They use their badges and boardrooms and company policies to cover their racism.

The black community has so many other problems that we are trying to overcome. These include Black on black violence, drugs, poverty, and broken families. The black community has come a long way over the years and we still have a ways to go. We are a strong people, a diverse people. We've been hit with so much and had to overcome so much that we have no choice. If you're strong, you survive. If you're not strong, you get eaten alive. I had grown up here. Sure, I see it all the time on the news and I knew it was happening and even happening here in my own city. I just never imagined that I would become a victim. The discrimination that I had faced with Fath Management was devastating, but police brutality was completely different. My fight with Fath had made me stronger than ever. I was more than prepared and willing to take the Cincinnati Police on. I was going to fight. I wasn't going to be broken and defeated and I sure wasn't about to let this drop.

"We Must Never Give Up!"

Chapter 15

Court Case

James Ludwig had discovered more information concerning my case. Fath Management hired Dan to take over my job in February 1994 as a Maintenance Supervisor. In 1994, he was hired with a gross bi-weekly pay of $1,346.00, which was about $16.83 an hour. By August of 1996, his gross bi-weekly pay was $1,538.00, which meant that he was making at least $19.23 an hour. My attorney was really doing his homework. I couldn't believe it. I had raised the performance level of that company's maintenance department in a matter of only 6 months and I was doing it all while working for peanuts compared to what they were paying this man. They were paying him more than me, and he had minimal maintenance knowledge. This was the same guy who once told me that he only knew woodwork. I could not believe that he had gotten the position. He also admitted that his old lifelong friend Larry, who was a manager at the corporate office, helped him to get the job. I thought about the $8.75 an hour that they were paying me to supervise all three properties. The thought actually made me sick to my stomach. This is just one example of exactly why we still need affirmative action. We've come a long way, but we still have so much further to go.

The information I had been receiving was overwhelming! Fath and their attorney decided that they wanted me to see one of their doctors to have my I.Q. tested. Can you believe that? They actually wanted me to take an I.Q. test! Aren't blacks intelligent enough to run their company? My attorney and I knew that this was irrelevant to my case, but he advised me to take it anyway. After I took the test and the results came back, Fath and their attorney wanted me to take another one. Fath said that their doctor had given me the wrong I.Q. test. If that was the case, maybe it was their doctor who needed to take the test. Maybe they had the wrong man working on their team (If he wasn't bright enough to give me the right test, what made him qualified enough to give his professional opinion as to whether or not I was intellectually capable of management?). I humored them and took another test. Besides, my court date was fast approaching.

The Black Positive Brothers and Sisters organization was slowly deteriorating. Some of the members were losing their focus while others just didn't have the time anymore. One of the biggest problems was that we couldn't get enough support from our black communities. It was pretty much over for Black Positive Brothers and Sisters. The organization had done a lot of good for a lot of communities, but I was getting burnt out and couldn't do it much longer. We couldn't even get the consistent support from the parents whose children were in our Youth programs. I hated to see it end, but it was over. Even though Black Positive Brothers Sisters had ended, I continued working with and talking with the youth. I still occasionally visited the schools and talked to different classes. Black Positive Brothers was still in my heart. It always will be.

In March 2001, the Office of Municipal Investigation came back with their findings on the investigation in regards to my complaint against the Cincinnati Police Department. Their conclusion was that the Cincinnati Police did indeed do me an injustice. O.M.I. found that the evidence was sufficient to substantiate discourteous treatment by the police. They found that the police should have given the names and badge numbers of the initial officers involved. They also found that there is no requirement that a citizen file his complaint with the supervisor on the scene. They recommended appropriate disciplinary action against the police officers for improper search and for the discourteous treatment. They noted that there had been five complaints filed at O.M.I. against one of the initial officers in the last 19 months. The O.M.I. report was signed by the City Manager of Cincinnati; John F. Shirey.

This was the backing I needed in order to take the police officers to court. I planned to file suit against the officers and the City of Cincinnati. We should always remember that if we handle a difficult situation the right way, in most cases, justice would prevail. One of the things I was taught, as a child is that it's all right for you to stand up and fight for yourself. And if you do it in the proper manner, you're likely to go much further. It's important to go through the proper procedures and file a complaint. If there's no action, things will never change.

Kenneth Lawson was an old schoolmate that I had grown up with in the "hood". Today he is a prominent attorney in Cincinnati. I paid Ken a visit to discuss the O.M.I. report. After reading the report, Ken agreed to take my case. He was really upset about how I had been treated. He said that he was tired of the mistreatment of African-Americans at the hands of the Cincinnati Police Department. Ken filed a suit against the Cincinnati Police Department and the officers that were initially involved in the case. My court case was scheduled for August 2001.

October 2000 was the month that I had been looking forward to for quite some time. I was finally going to have my day in court with Fath Management. I was a nervous wreck the whole day before court. I didn't get much sleep that night either. As a matter of fact, at about 5:00 a.m. I got up and went to the gym for a workout. I lifted some weights and followed that up with a quick run. After taking a shower at the gym, I put on my suit and tie and headed off to meet James and his assistant for breakfast. After breakfast, we headed off to the courthouse. Win or lose, I knew that the outcome would be God's will. I was confident that I would win though. How could I not win with all the evidence and facts that I had against Fath Management?

Jury selection was the first step. As it turned out, all the jurors were white with the exception of one black woman. I thought to myself, what was I going up against? My witnesses were all black and had worked for me when I was with Fath. Only one of them was still working for the company. Fath had to prove that I was not a supervisor and that they had done nothing wrong. All of Fath's witnesses were white and most of them were managers.

Once the testimony started, I couldn't believe what I was hearing! I couldn't believe that these people were willing to face perjury charges and penalties for this company. I had never heard so many lies in such a short period of time in my entire life! Each and every so-called witness testified that I had never been a supervisor and that I had just been given the responsibilities until they could find someone qualified to do the job. My attorney entered the newsletters written and printed by the company for evidence. These newsletters said that Charles Wiley had been promoted to Maintenance Supervisor. My attorney even presented proof that the owner himself had sent me a birthday card and inside in his handwriting it said "Congratulations on your new position as Maintenance Supervisor". My attorney showed Jerry, the manager, some documents that he had signed that stated I was a supervisor. Jerry looked at the documents and said that he didn't recall signing them. My attorney tore them and their lies apart. They had all sat on the stand, pledged to God under oath and lied with no remorse at all. Unbelievable!

Later that day, my witnesses came into the courtroom and took the stand. They all testified under oath that I had been the supervisor and that I had done a great job. They confirmed that I ran everything at 100%. Then it was time for Lou to take the stand. Lou still worked for Fath and had everything to lose. He held his ground though! He didn't back down. He held up his hand and swore to tell the truth and he did just that. I was so proud and grateful for Lou knowing that he depended on Fath to pay his bills. When you stand up and speak against the company that signs your checks knowing that there could be consequences, but you speak anyway, that says a lot about a persons dignity and honor. These are two qualities that were obviously missing from Fath's witnesses.

The next witness my attorney called to the stand was Dr. Thomas. He testified that I had experienced significant depression, anxiety and stress related to my job situation. His testimony was brief, but effective. It was now time for me to take the stand. I told the jurors that I had been promoted to Supervisor and that I ran the entire maintenance crew. The manager and I had signed papers for the position and a pay raise was supposed to start right after I took the position. I told them that the company had used me because they knew I could get the company where it needed to be. Furthermore, after the company had gotten what they wanted out of me, they treated me like I was less than a human being.

After my testimony, Fath's doctor took the stand. He told them about the I.Q. test that I had taken. Basically, he said that I didn't have the intelligence needed to run the maintenance crew. I thought to myself, "it wasn't enough that they had humiliated and embarrassed me, but now they were calling me an idiot". It didn't matter though. Fath Management wasn't smart enough to cover their behinds and now they were sitting across from me in Federal Court.

I always told my son and the youth that I worked with that you don't have to be the smartest person to be successful. With a little book smarts, street smarts, common sense and some hard work, they could become anyone and do anything they wanted to. I told them that their skin color means they would have to work twice, sometimes three times as hard as their white counterparts just to be considered as good as them. Life isn't always fair, but we must continue to do our part to help this society so that one day, hopefully, things will become fair.

The entire trial took about 5 days. To my disappointment, the jury had been in deliberation for only about two and half-hours before they came back with a verdict. I had waited for almost six years for this and it was all about to come to a very quick end. We were called back into the courtroom and stood anxiously awaiting the decision.

The lead juror stood up and slowly said that on the charge of discrimination, Fath Management was "Not guilty". I immediately looked over at my attorney James Ludwig. He looked back at me with almost as much disappointment on his face as I had on mine. He than gave me a hug and I thanked him for his representation. I didn't understand. Everything seemed to be in my favor. **James asked the judge if he could ask the jury what their decision was based on. After the judge approved this, the jury said that management had been at fault, but that the company itself was not. They said that it was a case of mismanagement.**

After the decision, the attorney for Fath walked over to me and held out his hand as a polite gesture. I shook his hand. He said, "Charles, you are a good man." The entire time we were going through this drama, he never had a kind word for me, but now that it was over and he had won I was suddenly a good man. Yeah right! My attorney said that I could appeal the decision if I wanted to, but I would have to take on most of the cost myself. I told him that it was over and I thanked him for all his support. He had done a great job. James had worked long and hard over the years preparing my case and now it was over. You would have thought that I would have had a melt down over the loss, but I didn't. This was God's will.

I left the courthouse and called Tracey. She had dropped me off at the courthouse so I didn't have a ride home. I told her that the case was over and she didn't need to come and get me. I was going to ride the metro bus home. She really wanted to come downtown and pick me up, but I really needed time to myself, I really needed to think. I told her that I was going to ride the bus to Reading Road in Roselawn and that she could just pick me up there. She asked me about the case, but I told her we would discuss it when she picked me up. I hadn't told anyone that the case was going on except for a few family members and close friends. But I had to wonder: where were the media and newspapers while this was going on? Fath Management was no small company. This was a big court case. Harry Fath owns properties all over the United States. My battle really wasn't about the money! I wanted this case to be heard. This kind of discrimination needed to be stopped. I wasn't only standing up for myself, but I was also standing up for each and every one of my people who had been treated in this manner. What just happened? Not only had I lost the case but also the public and our communities would never know what type of company Fath Management was.

I lost! I lost! I lost! God, I just knew that this was your will and that I would win. When I got off the bus, Tracey, Anthony and Serenity were waiting for me. Tracey asked me who won. After I told her, she said, "no they didn't!" I guess she expected me to be broken down because of the outcome of the case. I think she was a little surprised by my attitude. Tracey and Anthony gave me big hugs and we drove home. Throughout the ride home, the trial was on my mind. This just wasn't right with me. It was as if the last six years hadn't happened at all.

My spirit was low. I didn't want to do anything but lie on the bed and stare at the ceiling. I just couldn't put the case behind me. I wasn't angry or upset; I just really didn't understand what had happened. How could the jury have reached this decision? How could the company not be responsible? Companies have always been responsible for their management team; they're the ones doing the hiring.

It was about 6:00pm and it was a beautiful day. Tracey was trying really hard to get me up and out of the house. At first, I just couldn't do it. But as I lay on the bed, I began to feel God's presence all around me. I felt so calm and relaxed. It was surely God who had moved me to get up from that bed. There was something that he needed me to know. Suddenly feeling hungry, I got up and went downstairs. While putting some food into the microwave with my left hand, I rested my right hand on top of it. My hand came to rest on top of a plaque, which was on the microwave. It was a plaque that I had been given back in 1998. The plaque read:

The steps of a good man are ordered by the lord
And he delighteth in his way
Psalm 37-23
Presented to Bro. Charles A. Wiley
June 21, 1998
You are a go-getter for God
Ebenezer Second Baptist church

At the time I received the award, I felt as if I didn't deserve it. I knew that I hadn't been the faithful Christian that I should have been. But when I took the plaque down from the microwave and read it, I knew that it was God and not my hunger that had gotten me up out of that bed. My mind went back to what the attorney for Fath had said to me earlier that day in the courtroom. He had shook my hand and told me that I was a good man. "The steps of a good man are ordered by the lord". Being a believer in God and knowing that he was directing my path, I felt humbled and honored. At the time, I didn't know what Gods' plans were for me nor did I know why I had lost the case. But I did know that it was God's will and that he was guiding my steps. I hadn't seen this plaque in at least two years and here it was on this very day. I went upstairs and knelt down beside my bed in prayer.

I thanked God for giving me my day in court. I also asked him to let me know what he would have me do because I didn't feel that this was over. I felt there was more. I ended my prayer and lay back down on the bed. I was very restless. I got up out of bed and went into the spare room that we used as an office. I don't remember what I was looking for, but I reached up on the shelf in the closet and pulled down a book. It was an autobiography. I lost my grip on the book and it fell to the floor. I reached down and picked up the book and a small card fell out. The card read: "JESUS IS THE ANSWER." I knew what my next step would be. God had given me my answer. Tears of joy were rolling down my face. I went back into my room and prayed once again. I thanked God over and over again for this personal blessing. I felt so blessed! God was telling me to share my story. It was so clear to me that I should put everything down on paper and I started writing that same day. God was truly ordering my steps. My story would be heard. I would get the chance to tell everyone exactly what had happened. My ordeal with Fath management wasn't going to remain a secret.

"African-American leaders in the city were calling for change."

Chapter 16

Rioting and Looting in Cincinnati

Over the years, the number of complaints brought about by the citizens of Cincinnati against the Cincinnati Police Department grew tremendously. The citizens were more than fed up with police misconduct and they wanted something to be done. And they wanted it done sooner than later. There were a number of different complaints: officers unnecessarily drawing weapons, racial profiling, harassment, and engaging in unnecessary use of deadly force, etc. And the list goes on. The relationship between the black community and the Cincinnati Police department was very distant, if not non-existent. There was no positive police/community relationship.

In 1999 a Cincinnati Police officer shot a young man to death at a traffic light. The officer claimed that the young man appeared to be reaching for something that the officer thought was a gun. The officer then fired into the back of the young man's vehicle, killing him instantly. In another incident the following year, a young man died in the back of a Cincinnati Police officer's cruiser after being forcibly restrained by the police.

Tensions in the city between the black community and officers continued to increase. In April of 2001, a 19 year-old young man was shot and killed following a foot pursuit by a Cincinnati Police Officer. The officer was trying to arrest the young man because of 12 misdemeanor charges and two outstanding warrants. The young man was unarmed. This was the final straw that prompted the citizens of Cincinnati to take to the streets in a peaceful protest to stress their frustrations with police brutality. The march started out peaceful, but it certainly didn't end peacefully. As night fell, rioting and looting began. I witnessed the devastation and destruction first hand. The streets were crowded with looters and protesters. Most in the crowd were young black adults, and our teens. They were breaking storefront windows, setting fires, throwing rocks at the police, stealing from stores, pulling people from their cars. It was sad, but an amazing sight. I had watched the LA riots on television, so I knew all this was possible, but I had never witnessed anything like this first-hand.

I tried to talk to some of the youth and explain to them that this is not the way to get the city's attention. I tried to tell them that there is a better way. These kids weren't even trying to hear what I was saying. They just looked at me with that "man please" look on their faces. Actually, this disaster did get the city's attention. In fact, it attracted worldwide attention. The people of Cincinnati were being heard! A friend of mine had this saying. It was short and simple, but effective, "unbelievable".

The looting and rioting went on for several nights. By the third night, the mayor of Cincinnati issued a citywide curfew from dusk to dawn. The curfew went on for five days. No one was allowed on the streets after 7:00 p.m. unless he or she was traveling to or from work. If you were caught on the street after curfew, you would be arrested on the spot, no questions asked. I guess the knowledge that you would be arrested didn't concern some individuals. During the five-day curfew, there were over 500 curfew violation arrests. Of course, most of the individuals arrested were African-American. Most argued that the curfew was only being enforced in the black neighborhoods.

After the curfew was lifted and the city and its citizens began to settle down, the African-American leaders in the city were calling for change. A citywide boycott was initiated. As a direct result, the city lost millions. For the first time in years, the city wasn't playing host to the yearly "Jazz Festival" and several other major events were cancelled.

My profiling case was set for August of that year. My attorney Ken called me into his office and told me that he, along with the Black United Front, were going to file a "Class Action" law suit against the City of Cincinnati and its police force. The Black United Front is a local organization formed to deal with some of the problems that the black community was facing. Racial profiling was one of the problems that the United Front was focused on. Ken asked me what I thought about putting my lawsuit against the city on hold and joining in with the "Class Action" lawsuit. I told Ken that I would be willing to do anything to help. This was an issue that was very important to me as well as to many other residents in the city. One week later, Ken and the Black United Front held a high-profile press conference. I was there along with three other individuals who had cases pending against the city.

On that day, the racial profiling class action lawsuit was officially filed against the City of Cincinnati and it's police department.

"It was God's way of showing me that you can't judge an entire group of people by the actions of just one."

Chapter 17

Venturing Out

My job at Metro Prop. Realty was going fine. The pay was good and my pay increases were fair. I had been talking to my wife about starting my own business. The job with Metro Prop. was stable, but after working there for five years, I had become bored and wanted to do more. I needed to do more. I might have felt differently if I still had the organization to fill my time, but this was not the case. I was still taking advantage of the reputation that BPB had established though. I was still helping kids when I could and talking with the youth when I had the time. I would also help other organizations out with fundraisers by allowing them to use the Black Positive Brothers name. Black Positive Brothers organization had a really good reputation around the city; so having our name behind other group's fund-raisers helped them out tremendously. These events were always successful.

Even though I was still doing a little community work, it just wasn't enough for me. I needed to do more. When Black Positive Brothers was up and running strong, there was plenty for me to do. There was always something going on. It was exciting working in the black communities. At one point, we were working on opening up a mentoring center that would carry the organization's name.

Unfortunately, at that time, I was going through my problems with Fath Management and I wasn't able to give the project my full attention. It just never materialized. I thought that if I could get the center up and running and establish some type of payroll for the individuals who ran and taught at the center, then I could keep BPB up and running. (We all know it's easier to get people to give their time on a consistent basis when they are getting paid to do it.) To have kept the members interested for as long as I did was a real blessing. As far as I am concerned, the organization is a part of history. I will never forget Black Positive Brothers & Sisters. I will have especially fond memories of our youth. After all, they are tomorrow's leaders. It's hard to be a part of something so wonderful and not miss it when it's over.

After much discussion, my wife and I decided that it was time for me to go into business for myself. When I step out to do something, it has to be done right or it can't be done at all. I set the business up as a corporation. I then purchased insurance, developed a marketing and advertising plan, and purchased uniforms. The marketing and advertising plan wasn't too difficult. I knew my plan wouldn't require a great deal of money. I came up with three solid advertising vehicles. The first of the three to be implemented were door hangers. I had door hangers made up with my business listed on them: "Quality Home Maintenance" (I designed the logo myself). Everything that I specialized in was listed on the door hanger.

Q – uality Control
U – nique
A – 1 Service
L – ow Prices
I – nsured

T – otal Satisfaction
Y – ou Won't Waste Your Money

❑	Ceiling Fans	❑	Leaks
❑	Light Fixtures	❑	Bath, Kitchen Sinks
❑	Switches, Outlets	❑	Dry Wall
❑	Door, Door Knobs	❑	Painting
❑	Cabinets	❑	Bath Vanities
❑	Faucets	❑	Floor & Repairs
❑	Roof Leaks	❑	Gutters

Any Home Problems Call:
Charles A. Wiley
Office:
Cell:

I was able to get my family and friends to help with the door hangers. They went from door to door and delivered the hangers, free of charge (When you're good to people, they are good to you). My sons and their friends even pitched in to help distribute the door hangers. I know what you're thinking, sons? Tracey and I took in a foster son who came to live with us when he was 13 years old and our foster daughter when she was sixteen years old. This was our way of giving back to the community and helping our youth. We really didn't think of them as foster children. We treated and loved them as our own.

Anyway, I still needed to figure out a way to get the word out to potential clients. I didn't have a huge budget so I needed to make sure to get the biggest bang for my buck. The best source that I could come up with was the yellow pages. This was the second of the three vehicles. It was by far my best choice. It was also the most costly.

That was okay though. I was confident it would pay for itself.

The third and final advertising vehicle was just plain old word-of-mouth. I had developed quite a few contacts over the years and thanks to BPB, my phone directory was unbelievable. I picked up the phone and made several calls to people I had met over the years. I also gave business cards to anyone who would stand still long enough for me to put them in their hand. Around that time, I purchased a full size white Ford Econoline 250 Van with two ladders on the top. I had my logo put on the side of the van. In 2001 I was officially open for business.

I had really enjoyed my job at Metro Prop. Realty. At Metro Prop. Realty, you were judged only by the way you performed. I was always treated well. The owner was a real stand up man. I was glad that I had the pleasure of working for a company that respected blacks and treated us as equals. This was another blessing from God. This was something God wanted me to experience. It was God's way of showing me that you can't judge an entire group of people by the actions of just one. I appreciate Mr. K. for "keeping it real".

On my last day at Metro Prop., the office manager and my co-worker took me out to lunch. At the end of the day, Mr. K. shook my hand and wished me luck. He thanked me for the good job I had done while there. That was it. I was on my way.

A couple of months had passed and my business was becoming more and more stable. It was a lot of hard work, but nothing that I wasn't accustomed to. Most of my business was conducted over my cell phone.

Typically, potential customers would call and leave messages. I would retrieve the messages and set up appointments for estimates. I was a one-man show. I was the crew, secretary, payroll, etc. You name it I did it. It was great! People who knew me from BPB were amazed that I was able to do so much. I had managed and led the Black Positive Brothers organization and now I was managing and leading my own remodeling business. What a blessing! Life was great and Tracey and I were really enjoying ourselves.

Our seven-year anniversary was coming up and we had made plans to take a cruise to the Bahamas. It was a five-day, four-night cruise with an extra day in Miami. We needed this time together. And we deserved to treat ourselves.

"We Must Never Give Up!"

Chapter 18

9 Lives

We were approaching a New Year and I wanted another motorcycle. This would be my fourth. While living at Sun Valley Apartments I owned a 750 1982 Honda. When we had our house built, I sold that one and bought a 900 Suzuki 1995 Racing Motorcycle. I kept that one for about a year and then replaced it with a 1200 Honda Goldwing. The bike was really nice. It was loaded. (Now that I think about it, I probably should have kept that one.)

Every since my early teenage years, I had always owned some type of two-wheel motor vehicle. Whether it was a moped or mini bike, it was always a big thrill to be out there riding with the wind smacking me in the face. After I sold my Goldwing, I replaced it with a 2002 Suzuki Intruder. The bike was lovely! It was silver in color and I ordered extra chrome to give it a really sharp look. I even treated myself to a pair of leather gloves, his and hers helmets and a black leather jacket with two white stripes on the right sleeve. No one could tell me anything. I knew I was cruising and doing it in style!

On the night of April 10, 2002, my cruising came to an abrupt end. I had only ridden the bike twice before this night. My business and family obligations had kept me from enjoying the bike as much as I wanted to. It was around 12:30 am and I was riding my bike up Summit Road. I'm not sure exactly what happened, but I think the back wheel of my bike ran over a large piece of gravel or maybe through some oil. In any case, I lost control of my bike and went flying over the handlebars. My injuries probably wouldn't have been so bad if I had actually put the helmet on my head instead of leaving it on the floor of my garage. I also left the jacket behind, which would have most likely prevented my arms from being all scraped and bruised up. I did however have on my gloves. A brother was just trying to be cool. All I remember now is that I was doing about 35 mph and then I was airborne.

There was a guardrail there, but I'm not sure whether I hit it or not. The driver of a passing vehicle came by and picked me up out of the ditch. He said that I appeared to be unconscious. I must have been in shock because he said that by the time he got to me I had jumped up. At that point, nothing seemed to be out of place or hurting. I was a little dusty and dirty, but that was it. My bike was a totally different story. It was completely totaled! I still tried to start it though. After we couldn't get it started, we just pushed it to the side of the road. The man asked me if I wanted him to take me home. I told him that I would appreciate it. Suddenly my body was engulfed in severe pain. I couldn't even stand on my own two feet anymore. My head and neck were throbbing. The kind stranger had to help me into the car. I was mentally and physically out of it. I couldn't even give the man directions to get me home. The best I could do was give him my telephone number and hope my wife was awake. He was able to reach Tracey from my cell phone and she gave him directions to our house. By the time I got home, it took both him and Tracey to get me out of the car and onto the couch in our living room.

Tracey was insistent on taking me to the hospital. I managed to open my eyes and told her that I would be fine and that I just needed to lie down for awhile. I was passing in and out. Tracey decided that this was another one of those times when I didn't know what I was talking about and she dialed 911. While waiting for them to get there, she changed me out of my torn and dirty clothes. The next time I woke up, policemen, fireman and my two sons were surrounding me. They were trying to ask me what had happened and where I was hurting. I was so out of it, I really couldn't tell them anything. They took me to the hospital where the doctors kept me overnight. The next day, they said that, aside from some pretty bad scrapes, bumps and lumps, all I had was a broken foot. They checked my head and neck for injuries but there was no evidence of spinal damage. Finally, they gave me the okay to go home.

The police had my motorcycle towed. I couldn't believe that I had totaled a brand new motorcycle. I wasn't even thinking about the fact that I could have been dead if it had not been for God's protection, again! All I could think about was my totaled bike.

That next day, I was sitting on the couch with my leg elevated when I realized that sharp pains were shooting down the length of my body. At first I thought that maybe it was coming from my foot, but then I realized that the pain started at the base of my head and ran down to my feet. I couldn't move my head. And this was too much pain for me to just have a broken foot. I told Tracey that there was something very wrong. You would think that I would have gotten up right then and there and gone back to the hospital, but I didn't. I sat there for a little while to see if the pain would subside. But it just seemed to get worse. A little while later, the telephone rang. It was the hospital. The nurse said that they needed me to come back to the hospital immediately. She explained that there was something wrong with my neck and that I needed to have someone bring me back out to the hospital immediately. Tracey drove me back to the hospital.

They kept me overnight once again. The next morning they told me that I had broken one of the vertebrae on the right side of my neck. They put me in this big crazy looking neck brace. My nephew Carlos came out to the hospital to sit with me for a while. I could tell by the look on his face that he was worried about me. He said, "boy you have to be more careful. Otherwise, I don't know what I would do without you". Carlos and I were more than uncle and nephew. We had grown up together. We were more like brothers, so I knew what he was talking about. We were on the same page.

It was now time for Tracey to take me home. She was quiet three-quarters of the way home. I knew what was coming next. Even though I was older than Tracey was and she was my wife and not my mother, sometimes she would forget those two little facts and transform into a mother hen. Well, here it comes. Tracey went off. "You're not getting another motorcycle, so don't ask, don't mention it, don't even dream about it because it's not going to happen! Me and your mother are not going to stand for it". I hadn't even been home from the hospital for two minutes. A brother had a broken neck, a broken foot and his bike was gone. Can't I catch a break? But you know what? She knows me too well. I was already thinking about getting another motorcycle. After our conversation, or should I say her conversation, I decided to just leave it alone for the time being. I figured that maybe in a couple of years after all this had blown over that I would approach the subject again. In the meantime, I would be shut down for five months or so.

All I could do was watch television or go to the doctor. I couldn't do anything unless someone came to get me. During the time I was incapacitated, I had a lot of visitors, but my two main partners Moe and Greg were my most frequent visitors. They would sometimes take me to my doctor's appointments. Sometimes they would take me over to another friend's house and we would all just sit around and talk. A couple of times the brothers set me up. They would get me over one of our friend's house and just talk about me like a dog. I was the butt of many, many jokes with those guys. Many times they had me laughing so hard that I would be in tears. There was one time in particular that I thought I would break the other side of my neck laughing so hard! I used to wear the real fitted shirts sometimes. You know the ones made with Lycra in them (Hey, I worked out and I had the physique). Anyway, one day we were all sitting around at Big Daddy's house when Moe said "Hey man, how did you get your baby girl Serenity's shirt over that big crazy neck brace?" That was one of many jokes that they used when they wanted to talk about me and my neck brace.

The pain in my neck was so severe that the doctor prescribed Vicodine. I knew that it was about time for a brother to get off of them. I was really starting to want them and I knew that wanting them and needing them were two totally different things. I knew that it would be really easy for me to get hooked. I decided to stop taking them completely and deal with the pain. It wasn't as bad as it had been. I had started to heal so the pain was subsiding.

My doctor said that I would need a lot of therapy, but everything healed just fine and I was back at work within five months, without the therapy.

I was driving to work one day and started thinking about the accident. I realized just how blessed I was. The doctor told me that I could have died at the scene. He told me I was a very lucky man. Thinking back, one of the officers told me the same thing at the hospital the day after the accident. It seemed like I had been blessed with 9 lives: 1st pneumonia as an infant, 2nd near drowning at Camp Joy, 3rd the car accident, 4th the night club fight where I was knocked unconscious, 5th getting beat with brass knuckles and a crowbar, 6th the stabbing incident that almost cost me my freedom, 7th the fight I had with a convicted murderer, 8th the gun one of his partners held to the back of my head, and 9th the motorcycle accident. I now realize that I've used up my nine lives. I know that without a doubt, God has had his arms around me for an entire lifetime. There have been several times when I could have lost my life and my sanity. But with God's grace and mercy, I recovered and came out even stronger.

God had truly been good to me. But why? I was flip flopping from church to church. I had spent my adult life going from Ebenezer Second Baptist to Revelation Church of God. I hadn't made a commitment to either church. I wasn't completely committed to living a life that was "Christ-like". I still loved to party and do the things that came with it. You would think that someone who had gone through so much would be more committed to God and the relationship that he shared with God. My answer was always "God knows my heart". I always knew that God had a special plan for me, but like most people, I was resistant and often ignored him. I was afraid that God's plan for me wasn't the same as my plan. My life was like a puzzle and I was just starting to place the pieces in their proper places. I wasn't sure about a lot of things in my life. But the one thing I was certain of was that I couldn't run from God forever. Sooner or later, he would touch me and when he did, it would no longer be my will, but God's will. There would be no looking back.

Hey, I have a question for you. How many hard knocks does it take to get to the center of a brother's hard head? I don't know either, but it must be a lot more than I've had. The summer was just barely over and it had only been six months since my motorcycle accident when I approached the subject of a new motorcycle with Tracey. She wasn't even listening to me. It was like talking to myself. I guess she finally got tired of me blowing wind. One day she turned around and looked at me and asked me "what part of NO didn't you understand?" "Are you crazy?" She told me that if I bought another motorcycle into this house, we wouldn't be together anymore. Well, whatever Tracey. I'm a man! Being a man, I did what a man would do. I settled for a 1993 Thunderbird. Boy oh boy was it clean and flashy. The owner had installed a ground effects kit around the body of the car. It was tight! I wanted this car. Tracey on the other hand felt that I had plenty of other toys to keep me busy. I had a 2000 explorer and more electronic equipment than the electronic store. Why did I need this car? Although she didn't like it, she disliked the idea of another motorcycle even more.

"The steps of a good man are ordered by the Lord."

Chapter 19

Hats Off to Charles!

It was October of 2002. I found out that my wife Tracey was planning to throw a 40th Birthday party for me on December 21st. In a way, I was looking forward to it. It would be nice to celebrate my 40th birthday with all my family, dear friends and people who had watched me grow over the years. But then again, Father Time was catching up with me. I had been thinking and talking about getting older and I really didn't know how to feel about turning 40.

Tracey had joined a small bible study group at work. They would have weekly study sessions during their lunch break. A good friend of Tracey's taught the class. Tracey frequently talked about what a blessing it was to have her friend teaching the class. I could really see the spiritual growth in my wife. This was a good thing because it helped her to deal with some of the personal challenges she had been facing. One of her biggest challenges was physical. Tracey had began to experience severe pain in her back. She didn't know where the pain came from but it may have been a result of a car accident she had been involved in about six years ago. Things had been pretty bad for Tracey. She was dealing with chronic back pain. The pain was so intense, that often times she would call me from work crying. She had been to the doctor so many times that I had lost count.

The medical people were stumped. And since they had not been able to find out what was wrong with her, they weren't able to treat her adequately. The best they could do was to suggest exercises. I don't know whether those helped or made it worse.

In November 2002, Tracey's back pain was so bad that she could no longer sit for more than 10 minutes at a time. She finally had to leave work and go on short-term disability. I myself had only been back to work for a short time. Because of the time I had been away from my business to allow my injuries to heal, I didn't have very much work lined up. Besides, people just weren't spending money in late 2002. There were talks of going to war and consumers were cautious. They were only spending money on what was absolutely necessary. The approaching holiday season didn't make things any better either.

Although things weren't great financially, Tracey was insistent on giving me this birthday party. This was something that she really wanted to do for me and she believed that I really did deserve it. (Besides, it wasn't like we were broke and she had already set aside the money a little at a time, so it was not coming out of the funds that we had to live on.)

The theme for the party was "Hats Off To Charles". Tracey sent out over 200 invitations. A lot of my old project buddies and former members from Black Positive Brothers and Sisters were in attendance. The party was unbelievable. It reminded me of the parties Black Positive Brothers and Sisters use to give. We would play our theme song "Ain't No Stoppin Us Now" by MacFadden and Whitehead, and have the best time. On the invitation, Tracey asked everyone to wear his or her best hat. A couple of Tracey's family members and friends decorated the hall and everything looked wonderful. Tracey had really done a wonderful job pulling this event together. The decorations were on point and the food was excellent! But the best part of the night was yet to come.

After everyone had eaten, my sons and Serenity had a special present for me. They came out wearing a pair of tan pants and white t-shirts that had the same picture on it as the picture on the front of the invitations. The three of them stood in the center of the dance floor as the DJ played "Zoom" by the Commodores. They started singing and performing a skit that they had been secretly practicing for weeks. Those who knew me growing up, understood why they chose "Zoom" and what it meant to me. Back in the day, "Zoom" was always playing, whether I was rolling in my car or chilling at the house (Even today, I still play it at home and in my car. That song is a classic and one of my favorites).

I think its fair to say that everyone really had a nice time. I gave Tracey a big hug and kiss and thanked her for all she had done to make the night special for me. Tracey has always been a fantastic planner. Even though her back was killing her, she gave me one heck of a party. People were still calling days after the party to tell me how nice everything was and how lovely my family was.

In early 2003, Tracey was still on medical leave from work and my business had begun to pick back up a bit. Things were still slow, but getting better. We had to borrow from our investments because our savings had dwindled. I had to resort to plan "B" with my business if I expected to keep it afloat. I had to move fast. In the past, all of the work I had been doing was strictly residential work on private homes. This work was slow, so I decided to start bidding on jobs for commercial properties. Metro Prop Realty was the first commercial property that I contracted work from. I was more than ready and everything was in order. My workers compensation, insurance and the fact that I left the company on good terms made it even better. This contract was a true blessing. Tracey's insurance company had just denied her claim for short-term disability.

The insurance company said that the information submitted was not sufficient medical reason for her to be compensated for her back problems. We couldn't believe it! Being the fighters that we are, of course we appealed this decision. The company said that it could take up to sixty days for us to receive a response. We had been through worse so this wasn't anything that we couldn't handle. We knew that God was on our side.

I got more sub-contracting work from other companies. Homeowners had slowly begun to call for estimates. Financially, things were heavy but this time was different than our Fath experience. This time, we both had more faith in God and didn't worry about our financial future. God had always been there in the past, and he's still there today. But I was still running. God was calling me and I was still going about Charles' work and not God's work. I was still doing "my thang".

Our faith remained strong despite another challenge. I had just earned a contract with my second commercial property. About two weeks later I had done about $1,500 worth of work in addition to purchasing all the materials for the job. I had a gut feeling that there was something wrong. The manager of the property seemed to be too secretive. For example, I was given a P.O. Box for the company address and I had to ask for the owner's name. To make matters worse, she constantly wanted to meet for business at different restaurants (Which I never did).

After finishing the work, I turned in my invoice. Not surprisingly, I was given the run around and never paid for the job. Timing could not have been worse considering what was going on in our lives financially. Did I happen to mention that this manager was a "sister"? She should know how hard it is for a brother to go into business for himself. You would think that I would not have faced this sort of problem dealing with a black woman managing a company. At any rate, I was forced to go downtown and file a small claim lawsuit against her company. I knew that this would be something small for me to handle. When you do the work correctly, you expect to get compensated. In this case, it didn't happen that way. However, with God's help I would deal with it as I usually did and definitely resolve the problem.

My final statement to reporters:
"Only time will tell."

Chapter 20

16 Suits Settled For $4.5 Million

In February 2003, I was on Northbend Road at the car wash. I ran Tracey's van through the car wash and now I was headed home. I looked both ways before pulling out onto Northbend Road. As I was sitting waiting for traffic to pass, I noticed a police car about five car lengths down, headed in my direction. There were also two other cars about a half-mile away approaching from the other direction. Traffic was clear so I started turning left into the inside lane on what was a four-lane road. The person driving the police car was a black female officer, and she wasn't paying much attention to traffic. I'm not sure what she was doing, but whatever it was, she was trying to do it while making a turn. It's a wonder that she didn't turn right into me. When she finally looked up and saw me turning into the inside lane next to her, she jumped (She jumped so high that she could have come right out of the roof of the car).

I knew it. Here come the flashing lights and sirens. I just knew that she wasn't going to try and find me at fault for this. I slowly pulled over to the side of the road. She was so nervous that she almost ran into the back of Tracey's van. While all of this was going on, I was having a conversation with Tracey (No, I wasn't using one hand to drive and the other to hold a cell phone. I was using the hands free earpiece). Anyway, the officer approached my car and in my nicest, non-threatening voice, I asked her "what's the problem officer?" She asked me if I had seen the two oncoming cars that had to slam on their brakes to avoid hitting me. The officer had no idea that my wife was on the other end of the phone and could hear the entire conversation. I looked at the officer with somewhat of a smirk, trying really hard not to laugh and I said to her "no you didn't go there." She ignored me and requested my driver's license and proof of insurance.

Oh no she didn't. Did I just see her whip out her ticket book? Why is she giving me a ticket? She was the one driving blind. This woman is actually going to give me a ticket! Unbelievable! She's giving me a ticket. All right, let me see if I understand this. She's giving me a $100 ticket for almost causing an accident. Who else was involved in this "near accident"? The only two people involved were she and I and she was the one who was at fault; she hadn't seen me because she was fiddling around inside her cruiser.

The officer finished writing up the ticket and asked for my signature. I asked her why she needed my signature. I told her I wasn't signing that ticket or any other ticket because I hadn't done anything wrong. I wasn't the one who had almost caused an accident. I could have let her know that it was her who almost caused an accident by not paying attention to the road. I also could have asked her how she could have possibly seen two oncoming cars through my big mini van. I didn't even go there. I knew that she was trying to bamboozle me, and I wasn't going to give her the opportunity to come up with a better story for court. Oh yeah, I was taking this to court.

The woman became angry and appeared to be embarrassed. She told me that I should have waited for the two cars to pass before turning into traffic. I told her that if that was the case, she could have sat out here all day long and given out tickets to nearly every other driver on the road. She said that I was right, but she was still giving me a ticket.

I once again repeated that I wasn't going to sign the ticket. I hadn't violated any traffic laws and there was no reason for her to be giving me a ticket. She told me that by signing the ticket, I wasn't admitting to guilt. In fact, that if I wanted to, I could go to court on the assigned date and dispute the ticket. She went on to say that by signing the ticket I was acknowledging that I received it. Again, I politely told her that I wasn't signing the ticket. What was her next response? You know what her response was. What are those eight little words that officers typically use as leverage? "If you don't, you will go to jail". Well, when you put it like that, of course I'm going to sign it. I wasn't trying to go to jail; I was just trying to get home. Man! You go to wash your wife's van and you end up facing jail time. I signed the ticket and went on my way, but I would definitely be in court on February 26th.

Tracey, my son Anthony and I went down to the courthouse on the assigned date. We were in room 134, Judge E.M. Cooper and our case was at 9:00 am. I was super nervous. It wasn't closed court where the only people in court were the actual participants. It was open court with a lot of different cases sitting around waiting to be heard. There were several officers in the courtroom and the majority of the defendants were black. Finally, the judge called me to the stand and it was show time. After being sworn in, the judge asked me to explain to her what had happened. I asked the judge if I could use the black board to demonstrate exactly what happened. After she gave me the okay, I explained exactly what had happened the way it had happened. By the time I was finished, the female officer was so embarrassed. When the judge dismissed the case, she was completely humiliated. Not only were the spectators laughing but some of her fellow officers were snickering.

When I walked out of the courtroom, people were outside the courtroom holding up their fist in the air and laughing. One guy said, "go ahead brother". Tracey called me Perry Mason. It felt good to stand up for myself and get justice. I was glad Anthony was with me. I took him to court with me for a reason. I wanted to let him know that you can fight back. I wanted him to know that there was a proper way to handle disputes when dealing with police officers or any person of authority. Don't ever let anger control you. Control your anger (I was speaking from past experiences). Even if this case hadn't been decided in my favor, I had stood up for myself. And you never lose when you stand up for yourself. I would have loved for my other son to have been in court with us. This was a lesson that he too could have benefited from. (He was in school taking care of business and taking advantage of everything that Tracey and I had taught him) Anthony had been able to attend the court session because he had been suspended from school for five days.

I just didn't understand Anthony. He constantly stayed in trouble with me because of his performance in school. No matter what I did, or how many of his privileges I took away, he just wouldn't do what he was supposed to do. There were even times when Tracey and I thought that maybe we were being too hard on him, so we would cut him some slack. This approach didn't work. He would just get into even more trouble. He was disruptive to the teachers and other students because he always did childish things. He wouldn't study and he would never complete all of his schoolwork. He just wanted to clown. I just could not get this boy to grow up and get serious. Ironically, his teachers often told Tracey and me how intelligent he was. He had passed all of his proficiency tests in the 9th grade, and we weren't going to give up on him. We were determined to find a way to reach him. We tried everything. From tutoring to counseling and we even signed him up for the Young Marines.

Anthony was not a bad kid. In fact, he's always been very respectful. He has never messed with alcohol or drugs and he's smart enough to do the work. His teachers said that part of his problem was his playfulness. Everything was a game to Anthony. You would think that after watching me go through all I had gone through, he would realize just how serious life is and that he needs to be prepared.

I had been grooming Ant to play basketball and football since he was about 4 years old. He was pretty good at basketball, but his real calling was football. He had an arm that was out of this world. By the time he was in 8th grade, he was the starting quarterback for his school's team. I myself stand six feet three inches tall and weigh about two hundred and fifteen pounds. I could tell that Anthony was going to be at least as big as I am and he loved playing football.

While Anthony was excelling at football, his grades were going south. He was barely making it academically. Ninth grade season would be his last year of eligibility for sports of any kind. Anthony's tenth grade school year really passed him by. His teacher once asked me if I thought maybe he was acting out because of our foster son being in our home? I knew that wasn't the correct explanation because we had been having these same problems with him long before Tracey and I became foster parents.

I just really didn't understand him. Some of our black males have opportunity after opportunity to find success and they don't even try. I learned a long time ago that we could do anything and all things through God. Growing up in a single parent household with so many other children in the house, it would have been really easy for me to just give up and settle. Giving up and settling just wasn't who I was. Tracey and I both knew that with God's help it would only be a matter of time before Anthony would be on track.

My deposition for the case against the City of Cincinnati was due in June of 2003. It was the early part of May when I received a call from Ken's office. He wanted me to come down to his office and meet with him. I was a little nervous. What could he possibly want to see me about? Ken and I met at his office and he had some great news to share. He told me that Cincinnati City Council would be voting to settle the 16 profiling cases with an offer of $4.5 million. He wanted to know how I felt about it and where I stood on a settlement. I was ready for the case to be over with. I had been feeling like my entire life was on hold so a settlement was just fine with me. I knew that dividing $4.5 million between sixteen people and lawyers wouldn't amount to much on an individual level. In addition, two of the sixteen cases were murder cases. That was okay though. The individual settlement amount wasn't important. When Ken handed me the papers, I quickly looked them over and signed them.

Cincinnati City Council held a special meeting on May 22, 2003 and voted 5 to 2 in favor of the settlement. This was the largest settlement in the city's history. The politicians knew what they were doing. They also realized that this was a very smart move on their part. They knew that if they had taken each individual case to court, it could have cost them a lot more than $4.5 million.

I think everyone involved was ready for this case to be over. We all wanted to move forward and it was hard to do that with the case still pending. I'm not just referring to the victims in the suit, but also the police officers, members of city council and the people of Cincinnati. This case was a big part of their lives too. I just hoped that everyone had learned from this, especially the officers. At the press conference held shortly after the vote, I made one final statement to reporters: "Only time will tell".

"We Must Never Give Up!"

Chapter 21

To God Be The Glory

One Sunday in June 2003, I decided to take my kids to visit Pastor Matt's church. Tracey's back was really hurting her that morning so she stayed at home. There was a female apostle who had spent a lot of time preaching in Africa present that morning giving the lesson. That morning, I questioned God. I asked him why I couldn't get motivated. Why didn't I have that thirst for him that some do? There were so many things that I had gone through and God had continued to bless me throughout. If not for God and his grace, I know I wouldn't have made it. Why wasn't I seeking him? Where was my desire? I thought about a guy that I met back in the 80's who gave his life to God after a really bad car accident and never looked back. Can I be that thick in the head? I go to church, I pray and I honor God, but I didn't have the desire to know him on a deeper level.

As the apostle was teaching, she said that one of the reasons that some of us are running from church to church was because we were still unsettled. She said that we need to first come back to God and then come back to church. She said that sometimes God might not be quite ready for you to be in the church at that time. I had to somewhat decipher the last thing she said. I understood it to mean that God wants all of his people close to him but as we all know, all of us aren't. Sometimes God will let us go through things so that we know it is him who carries us through. That way, once we come to know him and receive him in our lives, we will have more knowledge and power and we won't want to turn from him again. Her message really hit home with me. I found myself trying to hold back the tears. After all, I was a "strong man", and I didn't want my kids to see me cry. After she had finished her lesson, she asked if anyone wanted or needed prayer. She instructed us to come to the front. I could see Anthony out of the corner of my eye coming up from behind me. By the time I made it to the front, others were also coming up for prayer. She prayed for me first and I couldn't hold back the tears anymore. I asked God to come into my life and to forgive me for all of my sins. I re-dedicated my life to God. I knew that it was not going to be easy for me to put God's will first and what Charles wants second, but this was something that I felt strongly about. And I knew that God was calling me.

I never asked Anthony what his prayer was because I already knew the answer. At church on the following Sunday, Deacon Harrison was singing a solo. The selection was "He touched me". I had heard this song so many times throughout my life but it had never had as much meaning as it did at that point. I could feel God's presence.

On July 2, 2003 I was at Wal-Mart with Tracey and the kids. I was walking through the store by myself when I heard someone say, "Charles Wiley". When I turned to see who it was, imagine my surprise when I saw that it was Dan from Fath Management. He held out his hand and I shook it with no hesitation. I told him that there were no hard feelings on my part over the situation with Fath. You could see the relief wash over his face as he thanked me.

We talked for about ten minutes and he introduced me to his wife.

Dan told me that he had been keeping up with me over the years through articles in the newspapers. He told me he had been working for his brother doing remodeling work, but that he had to leave and take another job. The remodeling business didn't work out for him. He asked me who I was working for. Of course, I told him that I was self-employed and enthusiastically told him about my company. Dan went on to tell me that Jerry was worried about being laid off from his job. (Jerry was the man who had promoted me at Fath.) I thought to myself, "what goes around comes around". I actually held a conversation with Dan without once feeling any anger, grief or anything bad.

As I started to walk away, I thought to myself, "of all the people to run into at this time in my life". The timing was unbelievable. I had run into Dan during the time when I was putting the finishing touches on my book. Running into Dan made me think of how every incident in my life had fallen right into place one by one. I am now walking in God's path, wondering what my future holds. I'm not worried though because it is in God's hands.

To God Be the Glory

"WE MUST NEVER GIVE UP"

Closing Remarks

Growing up in poverty and going through the difficulties I have come upon in life have shown me just how precious life is and just how difficult things can be for our youth. Life can and most likely will be a lot easier for the person who chooses to continue his or her education after high school.

It is my belief that neither a person's education level nor their skin color should be a contributing factor when developing your opinion of that person. In life, everyone should be treated equally and fairly, regardless of his or her education or skin color. We are living in a society that tells us that the higher your education level and the more you know, the further you will climb up the corporate ladder. We have seen our brothers and sisters make it up that ladder time and time again, only to be reminded that they are still black.

We have been told so many times that we should forget what happened in the past and just move forward. But what they don't understand is that we could never forget our past. Our past is a part of who we are. Our past has made us the strong people that we are today. Besides, how can we forget what we stand and face every day in our communities? Some will say that if we don't like being here in America, then we can always go back to Africa. My response to those people is that we didn't ask to be brought here; you made the decision for us. Unlike my ancestors, I was born in this country. I am an American. I can only imagine just how wonderful a place Africa would be today if not for the interference of Europeans. What type of place would it have been if our ancestors had been left in their homeland, free from those who would enslave them and strip from them basic human decencies? The world will never know.

God has taught me not to complain or dwell on the past, but to stand up and do something to shape the future. Our youth need us and it is time for us to take a position of leadership and show them that we are there for them. This country is what it is today because of the great many contributions and hard work of African-Americans. White America would have you believe that we were mere servants and that our contributions to the building of this nation were very few. But we all know what the truth is. If we are going to make a change in this country, then black and whites are going to have to come together as one. This is what is most important to me.

In closing I want you to ask yourself this question: do you know the difference between being a racist and being prejudice? Which are you? Do these words apply to you? Can you honestly say that neither of these words describes you or your actions?

Sid was born March 4, 1963
He was shot and killed by a 17 year old African-American
male on October 10, 2003

"We Must Put Down The Guns"

We are losing too many of our brothers by the hands of gunfire. Are we not the MEN of yesterday that we can't settle our differences another way?

"Charles A. Wiley was a lead plaintiff in the historical racial profiling lawsuit that was filed in Federal Court on behalf of African-Americans that live or travel through the city of Cincinnati. I have known Charles since grade school and what happened to him at the hands of the Cincinnati Police is something that happens to African-American men and women everyday throughout the nation. Many do not have the courage to stand up and fight:some are mad for a week or two, but then they call me back and say that they don't want to file a lawsuit because they don't want to start trouble. Yet, Charles was determined to make sure he did his part in seeing to it that no other brother or sister would be put through the humiliating experience that he was put through for doing nothing but lawfully sitting in his own automobile."

"Charles has a way of describing what happened to him in such a way that you can feel not only his pain, but the pain our ancestors felt century after century, day after day, and it still continues."

"The beat goes on."

Kenneth L. Lawson
Attorney at Law

A short look back at Wiley v. Fath Management

"As the jurors made clear following the trial, Charles A. Wiley was wronged by Fath Management. Charles and I strongly believe that he was the victim of racial discrimination. The Jury, while they felt the treatment unfair, did not feel that it was discriminatory. I respect and understand that decision."

"Nowadays, discrimination comes not in the form of a blatantly offensive word or action, but more often in a form that is much less tangible. It is the type that can be felt through the senses rather than seen or heard through one's eyes or ears."

"I am proud to have represented Charles Wiley. He is a man of great character and integrity. A man that went through living hell, but never gave up and survived thanks to his own strength of character, as well as the loving support of his family, friends and Creator."

James D. Ludwig
Lyons & Fries Co., L.P.A.

"To God Be The Glory" by Mr. Charles A. Wiley, is an excellent memoir and guide for all people who want to overcome social injustice, emotional struggles, and spiritual confusion, in order to grow to the point where they, like Charles can give God the glory.

Charles, a job well done!

John H. Thomas, Ed.D.
Psychologist

I would like to thank the first two readers of my book for their inspiring comments:

This was a very interesting book. It was hard to stop reading it. It made me cry and laugh as I read the struggles of a young black man who grew up in my own town. It reinforced that I should not judge anyone because you never know what internal issues that they are dealing with. It was a delight to hear that even through his most difficult times, he sustained the faith of a mustard seed and Never Gave Up! This book can apply to many of our lives in one way or another. He made me take an internal inventory, recognize how blessed I really am and that we all are a part of God's plan.

---- Carmen Daniels

This book is more than one black man's story; it's an entertaining testimony on how God can speak to us and change us through different life events and challenges.

---- James T. Cowan, Marketing Professional

Watching my husband go through one unjust situation after another over the years was eating me alive. I would always feel helpless because there was nothing that I could do to ease my husband's pain. Fath Management truly did my husband wrong. The stress and turmoil seemed to increase for us. It was as if we were in a long nightmare. Knowing the type of man that Charles is, (a man with a lot of integrity, very intelligent, a very very hard worker, always willing to lend a helping hand to anyone, very outgoing and a good listener), you can imagine how it hurt my heart when I started seeing what they had done and were doing to him. He is a Black man with pride who always kept his head held high. They did almost strip him, but of course, they didn't.

Then there was the Cincinnati Police. I am glad I'm not a Black man because they really have it hardest of all races and genders.

Through it all, my husband has PREVAILED! One thing that we both did (especially Charles), was to keep faith in God and Never Give Up! Charles has endured so much in his life, so far, and for him to now be able to actually tell his story is just amazing to me.

I am truly proud of you and still continue to love you more and more each day. Even though you have nothing to prove to anyone, you have surely shown that you are a STRONG BLACK MAN that loves your family, community and country.

Much Love,
Your Wife